THE CHURCH COMMUNITY
LEAVEN & LIFE-STYLE

D0868917

THE CHURCH COMMUNITY

LEAVEN & LIFE-STYLE

MAX DELESPESSE

AVE MARIA PRESS / NOTRE DAME / INDIANA 46556

Originally published in 1968 under the title *Cette Communaute Qu'on Appelle Eglise*
© 1968 by Les Editions Fleurus (Paris) and The Catholic Centre of St. Paul University (Ottawa)

First English edition published by Novalis (Ottawa)
© 1969 The Catholic Centre of St. Paul University
Translated by Kenneth Russell

This edition published by special arrangement with Novalis (Ottawa). © 1973 by Ave Maria Press. All rights reserved

International Standard Book Number: 0-87793-057-0
Library of Congress Catalog Card Number: 73-80089

Printed in the United States of America

CONTENTS

INTRODUCTION

The solution to all the problems we face today: war, hunger, overpopulation, etc., depends upon the answer given to this question — how are men going to get together on this shrinking planet? The salvation men seek today is precisely the ability to get together in a way that will last. And we know, clearly or vaguely, that such unity and identity will not flow *automatically* from technical advance but that technology, by liberating men, is ultimately capable of either separating men from one another or uniting them. Everything depends on man's determination to seek out and meet his brother in an effort to share with him.

In this world seeking to unify itself, the Church claims to be the sacrament of the unity of mankind, i.e., it is at the same time the sign of and the means to this unity. What is the Church's vocation, what is its role in relation to this coming together of men in unity? We must ask ourselves two questions:

- In what sense is the Church a community? How does it unify the men who are its members?

- How can the Church, for its part, help mankind to become a community of communities and to find the unity it is seeking?

Certainly it is impossible to treat such a vast subject in a few pages. This small volume is only a sketch. Its aim is not to exhaustively and thoroughly analyze all the aspects of the community life of the Church and its presence in the world. I am prompted to write it because concrete experiences of life in a community have led a number of Christians, of whom I have the good fortune to be one, to look at the ecclesial reality in a manner quite different from that found in the cliches which are usually presented. And I would like to put forward their experiences, their intuitions, their convictions and their questions as well.

Experimentation and intuitions cannot be separated from revelation and Christian tradition. It is for this reason that we sink our roots into scripture and into the teaching of the Fathers as well as into the message of the Spirit to the Churches and the world of today. The reader, however, must keep in mind the exploratory character of this small work. We ask him to share his remarks and corrections with us in order to contribute to the construction of authentic communities within the Church both today and tomorrow.

Max Delespesse

CHAPTER 1

THE CHURCH
IS A COMMUNITY

1. What Is a Community? — A Definition

Before beginning any inquiry into the community nature
of the Church we must ask, "What is a community? What
are the characteristics of the human gathering called a
community?" There are a number of ways to answer.
We might, for example, study the works of the German
philosopher and sociologist Tonnies (1855-1936) who
is noted for distinguishing between "the two absolute
sociological categories: community and society." But we
might also interview members of communities or, more
precisely, people who claim to be living a community
experience or at least sharing certain community values,
compile their testimony and try to scientifically construct
from this base a definition of community. This second
choice is not without pitfalls since it presupposes that the
interviewers have a certain notion of "community."
Nonetheless it has the advantage of being based on the
kind of life men live today and on their daily experience.
We have, then, opted for the second choice.

But once again, who do you turn to if you yourself do not have any experience of life in a community or at least an idea of what a community is? The fact is that my friends and I have lived such an experience (life is the best teacher) and this has motivated us to read and think about the subject. Here then, before any investigation, is how we characterize a community. You will see that our inquiry served only to make what we had suspected more precise, at the same time adding some things that were indispensable.

A community is a union of human beings held together by an underlying principle. The underlying principle unites the members in their very persons and not only in their activities or material goods (the results of which are merely a society), and makes them come to know and love one another. This knowledge and love is concretely expressed in a sharing at all levels (spiritual and material), in a mutual support and in a certain common life.

The underlying principle may assert itself as given data; for example, children belong to a family without having chosen it, or it may be the result of a choice and a deliberate option, as when one freely embraces some religion. But in both cases the bonds uniting the members are shown by love; without that a community might exist externally for a time but it would never be more than a body without a soul.

Using our own experiences, reflections and studies as a base, we invited to meet with us a certain number of people who were obviously really living as members of a community, or at least coming close to it, and who were practicing some of its values. The first such community weekend took place at Saint-Denis, near Mons, Belgium, in 1966.

The task of the first weekend in the community was, among other things, to define community. To get to this definition, the participants who were divided into small groups were asked to answer two simple questions: "At what moment does a community come into existence? What appears to you to be the most important thing in community life?"

The spokesmen for each of the groups announced the results of the discussions before the plenary assembly. The office then devised a synthesis which expressed the essence of the definition. This definition was put before the assembly, criticized, amended and finally approved. It is, therefore, as faithful as possible to the thought shared by those present.

You might wonder why we bothered to define community. First of all, the members of such widely different communities thought that expressing their common reality would help them to understand and to live it better. Then, with so many movements, charitable associations and societies of all kinds, we needed to grasp and express more clearly what we were and what we were after, not in order to oppose others, but to show them, and ourselves as well, the characteristics of the community synthesis that we were trying to live.

Then, too, if we were to continue communicating with one another and with other people, and if we were to avoid the inevitable confusion of ideas engendered by an imprecise use of terms it was absolutely necessary for us to establish a common vocabulary in which the words "community" and "communitarian" would be given their full weight.

Preliminary Remarks

— Our definition of a community may appear to some to be too restrictive. We think it's better that way. A community is a synthesis and this is in danger of disintegration whenever one essential element is questioned. This said, it is clear that we recognize in many movements, charitable associations and organizations authentic communitarian values without, however, considering these as communities. Indeed they might use our definition as a key to discover what communitarian values they have and in what respects they are not communities.

— It is not our wish that this definition should discourage those who seek to be a community. Progress in the construction of a community is often slow and hard but isn't it a little more certain when we have an objective and realistic notion of the goal we're moving towards? This definition helped many of the participants in the study days at Saint-Denis to discover what they were still lacking.

— We wanted a definition acceptable to everyone — Christians and non-Christians. Some of the terms were meticulously chosen so that a member of any community could accept them and adopt them to his spirituality or point of view.

— Finally it was well understood that this definition was only provisional. It may well be that the pressure of events and the real life experience of communities will force its review. We put it forward, then, humbly. It does, however, have a special value because it is the product of many quite different communities gathered together for a sincere consideration of their common values.

The Definition

A community is an organic and stable fraternal association of persons accepting responsibility for one another, through sharing both what they are and what they have, in order to bring about the union of mankind.

Georges Lethe, the chairman of the study weekend on the community, gave some explanations of the principal terms of the definition. We repeat them here and add some others. Strictly speaking, we are not trying to define each of the elements of the definition but rather to show what they cover.

Fraternal Association

— The word "association" was chosen for the vagueness of its meaning. Quite correctly, it was left to the rest of the definition to delimit the association called a community.

— The word "fraternal" expresses a relationship based on a life principle common to all the members. Christians recognize one another as brothers because they live the same life of Christ and are sons of the same Father, God. They recognize members of non-Christian communities as brothers because they are convinced that whether these know it or not they share the same sonship and the same brotherhood as Christians themselves. Nonbelievers may perhaps be satisfied with a deep awareness of the brotherhood in which all men share by virtue of their common nature and condition, and perhaps they will also be satisfied with the pyschological, social or emotional motivations which prompt them to join themselves to this or that social group.

— The fraternal character of a communitarian implies, in our opinion, the need for the members to know and love one another profoundly. We refuse then to consider as communities those associations which are too vast to establish what sociologists term "primary relationships" among their members.

— Finally, by the word "fraternal" we wanted to show that what we call a community extends beyond the particular relationship which binds husband and wife together in the "family community."

Organic Association

— A community is a living body. In a living body the whole is more than the sum of its parts. A community is something superior to the totality of each of its members. It has its own existence, its own autonomy.

— Like a living body, a community is composed of organs and different members each having his own place and role as determined by the good of the whole body. The members of a community are not scattered rocks but rather bricks which, by their position and function, constitute a new structure. Members of a community are united, one to the other, to form a body.

— The organic character inevitably results in a serious and functional organization. This organization, however, remains flexible to allow the community to continually restructure itself as there is need.

— The community's organic character does not lead to the devaluation of individuals. On the contrary, because it is realized that their aptitudes, desires, and needs give each of them a special place and function, such characteristics are developed and brought to their peak. The good of the corporate whole fosters the good of each member.

— Because it is an organic and living association,

14

the community does not govern itself by laws but by a sort of inner fidelity called tradition. By choosing a leader or a leadership committee the community establishes guardians of this tradition.

— From Christians the organic character of the community issues from the Pauline theology of the body of Christ.

Stable Association

— A community is not an association formed by chance like prison camps or the underground units evident in time of war.

— A community binds men together for better or for worse. It implies fidelity.

— It is, however, able to split itself in a kind of cellular multiplication so as to give birth to other communities.

— And, even though it is able to welcome uncommitted members who join temporarily, it remains constant in its cohesion and inner fidelity.

Association of Persons . . .

Without wishing to define the term "person" we have used this word to describe the full dimensions of a human being, all his aptitudes whether ordinary or special and all their extensions (including his material possessions). While society normally considers man only as an individual and brings men together to share only certain activities and certain goods, a community takes him in his very being with all its extensions and helps the person to develop himself through a permanent sharing with others.

Realizing a mutual responsibility

— The acceptance of responsibility one for the other is not just mutual aid. It is the action by which each accepts his brother with all his riches and all his miseries.

— This unceasing action can exist only through a mutual knowledge and love which find expression in physical, moral and spiritual support (interpersonal criticism), reciprocal discussion, advice, encouragement, etc.

— It presupposes a very concrete shared life covering a long span of time including meals together and eventually shared projects, a confession of faults and a common prayer.

— A common life is quite a different thing from a certain number of meetings which group together activities and points of view rather than persons as such and which consequently cannot conclude in the acceptance of responsibility one for the other.

— It is through this common life and by the acceptance of responsibility one for the other that a real collective and personal responsibility will develop.

Sharing what they are and what they have

— Not only does each accept responsibility for the others but each shares with the others, both spiritually and materially. Each offers what he is to the others — his qualities, weaknesses, and his material goods—in such a way as to bring about the fullest possible equilibrium, an equilibrium which is the product not of tensions but of convergence.

— The sharing of what they have is only possible because they share what they are. The sharing of goods in a community can only be the extension of the sharing of persons.

16

— Sharing involves surrender, availability, and detachment from oneself and from one's possessions. Sharing is opposed to acquisition and precludes both the incentive to possess and the possibility of possessing.

In order to bring about the union of all men

Because it achieves unity, the community carries in itself the salvation of humanity. It points towards the goal. But to be realistic it must be conscious of this vocation and grasp that mankind is destined to bring to fulfillment the unity which the community expresses. Therefore it ought to open itself to all men searching for unity and seek with them the means to attain it. A community turned in on itself would repudiate itself and would no longer be a community.

— Granted that this universal character of a community can be expressed in different ways and in different degrees of intensity according to circumstances, it is nonetheless essential.

— Christians will understand this by deepening their awareness of the eschatological character of the Church and the universality of the salvation brought by Christ.

It may be that some readers are shocked by our definition of a community. We live in a world so socially fragmented that it is hard for us to picture what a community is if we have never had the chance to live in one. But most of our readers are experiencing or have experienced an authentic unified family life. This certainly is the best starting point for the understanding of the reality of the universal community.

The underlying principle which establishes the unity of the family community is flesh and blood and likewise the family spirit. On the strength of this underlying principle the members of a family are able to share

17

spiritually and materially "from each according to his capacities, to each according to his needs" and the individuals are united "for better or for worse."

In an analogous way every human community can exist and continue only by virtue of an underlying principle of unity: It may be belonging to the same tribe, even to the same village, or it may be the sharing of the same ideal which embraces and informs the whole of life. Think, for example, of the kibbutzim in Israel where so many Jews live happily because they are conscious of belonging to the same persecuted people and of working to establish their nation in the land that they consider their own. Obviously, whenever the underlying principle is endangered, whenever it is obscured or attacked, the community itself is in danger of perishing.

But does there exist an underlying principle of unity which is permanent, which surpasses the human, which has been sent to men by God and through which they find themselves reunited in a family of families?

2. The Church Is a Community Theologically

A perfect community

We must say that theologically the Church in its very essence is a community. Christ really takes hold of the totality of our being as well as all those things that express and prolong what we are, and all together we form one body animated by the same Spirit. In describing a community we came to the point of saying that it was an association of human beings on the basis of an underlying principle. Among Christians this underlying principle of unity is not of the natural order: It is neither kinship nor human ideology but a principle which comes

18

from God into the hearts of men in order that they might find themselves called together into a community of salvation, into a community which is, for them, salvation already present and which will be for them, in its fulfillment, final salvation. The underlying unifying principle which establishes the Christian community is the Spirit through whose work the Son of God was incarnated, by whom he was raised up from the dead and through whom God brought forth on this earth for his sake a fraternal people, which is his own body already living by his life. For the Holy Spirit is so powerful that the community (or, if you like, the community of communities) that he establishes in the midst of mankind is truly a body, the body of the resurrected Christ.

What is really called for here is the whole Pauline theology of the body of Christ. Is there any image better suited to describe the perfect community than that of a body moved by the same unique Spirit?

"Just as a human body, though it is made up of many parts, is a single unit because all these parts, though many, make one body, so it is with Christ. In the one Spirit we were all baptized, Jews as well as Greeks, slaves as well as citizens, and one Spirit was given us all to drink. . . . The eye cannot say to the hand, 'I do not need you,' nor can the head say to the feet, 'I do not need you.' . . . If one part is hurt, all parts are hurt with it. If one part is given special honor, all parts enjoy it. Now you together are Christ's body; but each of you is a different part of it" (1 Cor 12:12-27, passim). Thus in Christ, Christians are members of one another, each living and working for all and all for one.

We understand then that ". . . there are no more distinctions between Jew and Greek, slave and free, male and female, but all of you are one in Christ Jesus"

(Gal 3:28). "And in that image there is no room for distinction between Greek and Jew, between the circumcised or the uncircumcised, or between barbarian and Scythian, slave and free man. There is only Christ: He is everything and he is in everything" (Col 3:11). As a perfect fraternal community the Church necessarily abolishes in herself castes, racial barriers, and privileges based on sex. Where these continue to exist and as long as they continue to exist we can be sure the Spirit is absent.

More powerful than flesh and blood, more powerful than any human ideology whatsoever, the Spirit is at work in men who truly welcome it. The Spirit unites them, makes of many families one family, and weaves between men the bonds which necessarily result in proper human relationships and a spiritual and material sharing.

Because they encounter God in the vital intimacy of the body of Christ, the faithful encounter one another, they become little by little comprehensible to one another, they communicate the Holy Spirit to one another and together become the living reflection of the Holy Trinity on this earth. God the Similar and Completely Different shows himself in the similar and completely different life of the disciples of Jesus Christ.

Mary is the type of the Church as community. In her are incorporated both the community of hope of Ancient Israel and the community of salvation of the New Israel. On her the Spirit descended to bring about the definitive encounter between God and man, the encounter which continues in the Christian community. Mary, the first member of the body of Christ, helps the whole assembly of the faithful to receive the Holy Spirit as she herself received it so that it may form them into the body of the Savior.

An All-embracing Community

It would be wrong to think that the union of Christians in the one body of Christ is a sort of spiritual union which does not involve anything more than some mysterious higher part of our being. Nothing could be further from biblical thought and the Christian tradition. No fiber of the Christian, nor any part of what he has, escapes Christ or the community. And in it there is salvation, real freedom from the world and the human and divine fulfillment of the sons of God.

Unfortunately, we often construct a so-called "supernatural" religion for ourselves which unconsciously conceals a terrible lie about man and about God. We are "brothers in Jesus Christ," full of devotion and compunction, but that doesn't hinder us from unjustly waging war or from oppressing other Christians and leaving them to starve to death. And so nothing's changed. "The Church," as a good priest once said to me, "perishes by its inhumanity." That's just it. How well the solidly established structures hide the absence of human relationships, those relationships without which there is no incarnation, without which God cannot act! To settle this argument we often hear it asked, "What do you expect? Sure, the Church is divine but it is also human." True. Unfortunately, it is only the humanity of the Church that can reveal its divinity. The Church shows itself divine to the degree that it shows itself human. Its divinity cannot manifest itself other than in its humanity. And if this humanity disappears under the scrap heap of intrigue, red tape, pomp, wealth, honors, organizations, offices and waiting rooms, it is the

21

Church's divinity that is hidden and obscured. As the body of Christ, as *the* perfect community, the Church is, for Christians, the preeminent place for "primary relationships," that is, for person-to-person relationships in mutual understanding and love. We must take care not to think of the relationships between Christians as purely supernatural. Grace does not destroy nature, it presupposes it and, we might say, builds on it so well that it pushes nature beyond its own limitations.

Between Christians of the same community there are bonds of understanding, love and sharing which are all the more profound because they have been lifted up to the divine level. Someone might object that it isn't possible to enter into primary relationships with all the Christians of the world even though together we form part of the same body of Christ. That's true. But because of this life in Christ that we have in common, we will necessarily seek to know them and to share spiritual and material goods among communities. Let us not forget that, when the local community is assembled, it is the whole Church which is assembled in it, the whole Church of all places and all times. This theological truth necessarily tends to be concretely expressed in the reality of life. On the other hand, we cannot live in the worldwide Church of Christ unless we genuinely live in the small local community.

In a special way the sharing of material goods is a law of the Christian Church. *The Constitution on the Church* has already recognized that ". . . between all the parts of the Church there remains a bond of close communion with respect to spiritual riches, apostolic workers, and temporal resources. For the members of the people of God are called to share these goods. . . ." The conciliar text is not a treatise on political economy; it does

22

not distinguish property, usage, etc. It doesn't even define any doctrinal position — it puts forward arguments. But this apparently spontaneous argumentation is a revelation of the underlying mentality of the Church as a community. However, above all, the constitution *Gaudium et Spes* (no. 69) and the encyclical *Populorum Progressio* (nos. 22, 23 and 24) should be studied. We will discuss the meaning and various aspects of community of material goods later. Let us recall now only that a sharing on the level of persons precedes a sharing of things and that this can come about only because things are the extensions of people. It was because the first Christians were of one heart and one soul that they pooled their material goods for the benefit of àll.

The Church as Community Is a Goal

As a perfect and complete community the Church must be classified as an end in itself. Often I have been asked: "What's a community for? What are your communities aiming at?" These are awkward questions because a community doesn't exist principally to reach some goal beyond itself. Certainly it has the salvation of its members in mind but this salvation comes about through the very fact that the community is called together by Christ. Certainly it has in mind the gathering together of all men into unity but this goal is included in its very essence — which does not of course dispense with the need to express this by concrete acts and by practical efforts which may be very absorbing.

The Church as a community must be classified as an end not as a means (as are, for example, charitable or missionary associations). It is an end because it is the anticipation here below of the eschatological reality of

23

the Church. The community of the Church is the community of salvation. Salvation is in it because it is already the final assembly. And the more authentic it is the more it hastens to prepare the assembly of the kingdom of heaven. It is the realization of love, and love is its only end.

We know that the definitive community and definitive salvation will be attained only by the return of the Lord Jesus. But only those who work to come together, and who work to bring their brothers together in the present, will share in the final coming together. The eschatological reality of the Church does not exempt it from the manifestation of that very reality in this world. Otherwise eschatology would be only alienation and an escape. The mission of the Church is to be today what the kingdom of heaven will be tomorrow. This is why the Church has received the life of the Risen Christ.

The Church as Community for the Salvation of the World

The final act of the salvation brought by Christ will be the gathering together of the elect in the kingdom of the Father, and this final gathering together is pointed to and prepared for by the gathering together effected by Christian communities. Because sin divides men from one another and from God, the salvation which God brings consists in the bringing of men together. This is a fundamental biblical theme that we should often ponder. And when God assembles men together in a community of salvation, he doesn't do it only for those who are there, but for the salvation of all men.

Basically, men understand very well that the problem is to find a way to get together. The solution to all our problems — war, hunger and overpopulation — depends entirely on the answer that we give to this question: How do we achieve this kind of brotherhood? Some think that men will get together exclusively by their own efforts and therefore they confine themselves to a strictly temporal point of view. They're deceiving themselves, but their mistake is only a reaching out for something better that the community of the Church will reveal to them.

By revealing to the world some indication of what the kingdom of God will be, something of the goal to be attained, the Church can inspire styles of life which are more communitarian and less out of step with the goal aimed for. If the Church is what it ought to be, men should discover in the way Christians live together, open to all their fellow human beings, a light for the organization of the secular city itself. In this way the Church can start to hand on to all men Christ's salvation. We will have the opportunity, later on, to develop these insights.

Certainly there exist, outside of Christianity, communities which from a certain point of view might be called communities of salvation. Salvation on the level of this life is a real salvation which does not in any way deny the doctrine of Christ, quite the contrary. Indeed the underlying principle which supports these human communities consists of human relationships animated by a human ideology. These communities are eminently respectable and valuable experiments and they show the profound needs of men. They are a great call to that irreplaceable supplement of the soul that only the Spirit of the Risen Christ can give. They live, awaiting the plentitude of the Spirit, to become with us the body of Christ, the Church.

Conclusion

We ought, then, to assemble to hear the word of God and to celebrate the Eucharist — it is there that we find the principle of our unity. But we should also assemble to live together in faith, in Christ Risen and present among us; in the expectation of his return and of the final gathering together; in the love which joins us to God and to one another; in a poverty which makes us share the goods of this world because we are conscious that we all participate in the same ultimate good — the kingdom of heaven. It is only in doing this that we will say "yes" to our ecclesial vocation and become a light for the world.

3. The Church Is a Community Historically

That the Church is a community is a theological fact. But is this fact evident in history? Yes, certainly. History proves to us that from its birth and throughout its existence the Church has been conscious of a call to be a community. Not that it always and everywhere has been faithful to its vocation . . . far from it. Nevertheless, the first three centuries show us the Church's authentic communitarian nature. And, despite its social fragmentation, the Church has preserved many communitarian values. All of its reforms have come from communities or have led to a community life. Unfortunately, we must be very schematic. Indeed, as astonishing as it may seem, Church historians have not shown much interest in the problem of the Christian community as such.

The "Apostolic Life"

To begin at the beginning, Jesus lived a community life with his disciples and the holy women. They even had a common purse which was entrusted to Judas Iscariot. This little wandering community formed of ordinary people, Galileans for the most part, assembled in itself the remnant of Israel and made it the people of the new alliance. Jesus came "to gather together in unity the scattered children of God" (Jn 11:52). But official Judaism, ossified, legalistic and proud, did not welcome him because it would not accept being gathered together by a Messiah who ate with sinners, who let prostitutes come near him and who violated the established order: "Jerusalem, Jerusalem, you that kill the prophets and stone those who are sent to you! How often have I longed to gather your children, as a hen gathers her chicks under her wings, and you refused! So be it! Your house will be left to you desolate. . ." (Mt 23:37-38). But the gathering together did take place in the assembling of a few men and women around Jesus. The death of Christ caused the disintegration of this group, but his resurrection revivified it forever through the Spirit.

Certainly to the Jews this community which came from Galilee was not such an extraordinary thing. Many pious Jews had lived and still lived in a similar way. This does not alter the fact that the communitarian character of this first group of disciples was explicitly willed by Jesus and that it was at the very center of his message; that he taught as much by the way he lived and the new style of life that he created among his followers as by his words and miracles. This life style of Jesus and his disciples was, moreover, exceptionally successful. At the outset it was this community that the Church in

27

Jerusalem wanted to continue as we will see next. This community, which people took as their standard in the first centuries of Christian history, was the origin of many reforms and very early its style of life was called the *vita apostolica,* the apostolic life. All of this demonstrates to us the importance which the primitive catechesis and Christian tradition attributed to the communitarian style of life which Jesus established.

The Primitive Community

After Pentecost the Jerusalem Church spontaneously set itself up as a full community, uniting persons and goods through the dynamism of the Holy Spirit. It is not a waste of time to quote here two well-known passages from the Acts of the Apostles.

These remained faithful to the teaching of the apostles, to the brotherhood, to the breaking of bread and to the prayers. The many miracles and signs worked through the apostles made a deep impression on everyone. The faithful all lived together and owned everything in common; they sold their goods and possessions and shared out the proceeds among themselves according to what each one needed. They went as a body to the Temple every day but met in their houses for the breaking of bread; they shared their food gladly and generously; they praised God and were looked up to by everyone. Day by day the Lord added to their community those destined to be saved (Acts 2:42-47).

The whole group of believers was united, heart and soul; no one claimed for his own use anything that he had, as everything they owned was held in common. The apostles continued to testify to the resurrection of the Lord Jesus with great power, and they were all given great respect. None of their members was ever in want, as all those who owned land or houses would sell them, and bring the money from them, to present it to the apostles; it was then distributed to any members who might be in need (Acts 4:32-35).

The exegetes have said all there is to say about these passages — that the Jerusalem experiment could not last. How do they know? In addition, Paul had to organize a collection for this community whose economic situation had become catastrophic. This can be understood if we recall that many Jewish Christians going on a pilgrimage to Jerusalem used the resources of the community during their visit. On the other hand, we can realize that the first thrust, inspired by the supposed imminence of the Parousia, somewhat lacked rational reflection and organization. This does not take away anything of its authenticity or its normative character for a life lived according to Christ. What the exegetes, in my opinion, have neglected to do is to reinsert these pericopes in the context of the traditional catechesis of the Church. We will perform this small task when we speak of the community of goods. We will see that a fresh historical investigation proves to us that this catechesis taught the full communitarian character of the Church as self-evident. When the author of the Didache, for example, writes at the end of the first century: "You shall possess everything in common with your brother . . . if you share immortal goods with one another, how advantageous will it be to also share perishable goods," it is clear that he is talking about the norm of life

29

customary in the Eastern Churches. The passages from the Acts of the Apostles, then, form only one witness among others of a traditional practice and catechesis.

Consequently, when the Holy Spirit descended upon them, the disciples spontaneously united in a community in the full sense of the word. It was certainly not by chance — that in so doing they wanted to correspond faithfully to the intentions of the Lord Jesus. And after the establishment of the community in Jerusalem, doesn't it seem that the same style of life spread everywhere although in different forms? On the level of human motivation it is without doubt its communitarian character that determined the extraordinary expansion of Christianity into the socially fragmented Greco-Roman World. "And there are no more distinctions between Jew and Greek, slave and free, male and female, but all of you are one in the Lord Jesus." Despite many difficulties primitive Christianity achieved the miracle of a community. It is not surprising, then, that the socially fragmented and divided world felt itself shaken.

Before moving on we should glance at two passages of the Acts of the Apostles and highlight some of their characteristics.

The pooling of goods carried out radically was second to the pooling of persons. Both texts mention this first. The "fraternal communion" of Acts 2:42 signifies the union of spirits and hearts and solicitude for the poorest. As for the second pericope, it starts explicitly with these words: "The whole group of believers was united, heart and soul" (4:32). The community of goods is not then a communism imposed from outside or in the name of a human ideology, but an expression of the love in which men are united. This oneness of men exists nowhere without the action of the Holy Spirit and is sustained only by "the teaching of the apostles . . . to the breaking of bread and to the prayers" (2:42).

The satisfaction of the needs of each individual is the principle governing the pooling of goods. In the primitive communities, the adage taken over by the French Communists: "From each according to his capacities, to each according to his needs" was fulfilled.

Finally, let us note how in such an atmosphere the apostolic work found its true setting: "They sold their goods and possessions and shared out the proceeds among themselves according to what each one needed" (2:45); "it was then distributed to any members who might be in need" (4:35). They lived a love truly incarnate and in conformity to the communitarian directives of the Lord and therefore Jesus himself made his community of salvation grow by adding new members to it each day. Certainly the disciples proclaimed Jesus Christ by word, but the Lord himself gave the increase primarily because they lived in conformity with his teaching.

For how long was the Church taken as a whole as much a community of communities as it might be? The epoch of the integrated Church lasted roughly until Constantine (312 — Edict of Milan). There were fraternal communities in which there were various offices (episcopate, priesthood, diaconate, etc.), but the holders of these offices did not set themselves apart from others and most important of all they did not form a privileged class. The communities respected and honored the charisms of each individual and so they included some virgins, that is, people vowing their celibacy to the Lord, who were not however cut off from their brothers because of this, even when a special residence was set aside for them. The pre-Constantine period deserves our continued reflection for, whether we like it or not, we must return to a life similar to that which developed at that time. Today we are, in fact, in a situation rather similar to that of the pre-Constantinian Church — we are a minority in an immense world, only this time it's a secularized world. It was not for nothing that many bishops declared after the Council: "The Constantinian age is finished once and for all." It is true, but we have to outline the consequences. The Church of the 21st century will be made up of integrated communities, for every community is necessarily integrated, i.e., formed of brothers having different offices and charisms but being, above all, brothers together.

The Formation of Communities Alongside the Ordinary Church

Twenty or 30 years before the Edict of Milan, but especially after it, some Christians responded to the incipient "decommunitarization" of the Church by the formation of groups of cenobites (later called monks). These elite souls wanted above all to rediscover the *vita apostolica* (the apostolic life) and the primitive *koinonia* (community).

We see then a sort of split in the Church. There was the ordinary Church which let itself be departmentalized, adopting even in its liturgy and style of government the customs of civil society, the Church becoming too much of a spiritual empire, the Pope becoming the spiritual double of the Emperor. This was the Church in which basilicas were constructed on the pattern of the imperial basilicas — and we pass from the "community that comes together at Cecilia's house" to great anonymous assemblies. Despite the beauty of a catechesis able to develop from now on in full freedom, and despite the development of a certain flair for liturgy, the Christian Church was submerged by the massive entry of the pagans; less and less it brought persons as such together, and more and more brought people together for the sake of doing certain things.

Alongside this ordinary Church there grew up a Church of the perfect — people who, not finding their place any longer in a departmentalized and in a certain way secularized Church, went out into the desert (in general this wasn't too far because they worked for the poor and they had to pay taxes) to form communities there. The bishops approved and so did the faithful. This doesn't stop us from witnessing a curious phenomenon. These people often lived without a priest to celebrate the Eucharist and gave themselves structures different from those of the ordinary Church. In other ages such innovations would perhaps have been considered a schism. . . . Strictly speaking then it was neither chastity nor obedience nor even poverty which was the peculiar characteristic of the social order visibly fulfilled in the gospel.

It was a fortunate split, all in all. In fact, from Constantine to our own day the cenobitic life, the monastic life and later the religious life maintained the intensity of the primordial communitarian character of the whole Church of Christ, although this has been done in an exclusive fashion because they have been too much on the border of ordinary Christian life.

The Beginning of the Middle Ages

After the critical period of the barbarian invasions

33

the Church succeeded, thanks especially to the monasteries, in giving a certain communitarian character to society, although an imperfect one in many respects. The beginning of the Middle Ages was a Christian epoch of a classless alliance of men, without states in the proper sense of the word and with an economy based on need. Except for the first term, it was this state of affairs that the weakened Christianity of the contemporary period met in black Africa without being able to understand or assimilate it. It is the same something beyond "societies" that many nations are seeking in a Marxist utopia unable as they are to find it in our decadent Christianity.

Reform and Renewal

The monastic reforms, like all the other efforts of renewal in the Church (canons, mendicant, third orders), have been undertakings in an unceasing search for the primitive *vita apostolica*.[1] Many others fell into schism, then into heresy (for example, the Cathars), because, among other things, the Church did not really understand that they were seeking authentic values and a return to the sources.

The Familial Communities

The familial communities of France (often associated with monasteries), the Slavic village communities, etc., impregnated with Christianity (but separate from the Church), enabled Europe to surmount the great crises of its history (the fall of the Merovingian Kingdoms, of the Carolingian Empire, the Hundred Years War and the great plagues which turned Europe into a graveyard). We have only started to study the history of the familial communities of France scientifically — some survived for two or three centuries, others lasted almost a thousand years. Not everything about them is edifying — the spirit in which they lived is not always that which we would like to see animate Christian communities today. But that did not keep these communities, where a family spirit, collective interest, attachment to the land, charity towards the poor and the fidelity to the Christian tradition blended together, from being for the West an important element of equilibrium and development in the midst of the tremors of history.[2]

The Republic of Guaranis

We must mention certain singular and extremely impressive achievements where a completely authentic Christianity was led by circumstances to organize and stimulate the life of a people and succeeded in creating a "new world" as it was called, or kingdom, which was a real fraternity on all levels. I mention in particular the Christian communist Republic of Guaranis (1610-1768). Leaving aside all the polemics about this formidable achievement alongside of which the kibbutzim of Israel appear paltry (because the experience at Guaranis was the work of an entire people) we must turn to history and not to novels or plays if we wish to make judgment. This history has been written by Father Lugon, and we advise our readers to refer to this author's excellent study.[3] You will understand why a French economist could say, "If they had given the Jesuits a free hand in Paraguay, Latin America might be right at this moment the most developed continent in the world."

Communitarian Renewal Today

Today the Church is certainly tending to become

again a community of communities. In all the countries of the world we see Christians grouping together into small communities, tailored to human dimensions. This phenomenon appears on the infra-parish or para-parish level. All the associations of Christian-neighborhood "communities," groups of families, "community organizations," some sectors of Catholic action which bring together husbands, wives and children, are not necessarily communities yet but they are moving in that direction. We must add to this the continually increasing number of communities in the full sense of the word which implies both a spiritual and material sharing.

Let us note some qualities of this basic "communitarization."

- The groups which establish themselves want to remain tailored to the human dimension — at any cost, there must be interpersonal and primary relationships (which presuppose mutual knowledge).
- These fraternal relationships (stimulated certainly by the grace of God) have a tendency to show themselves even in the material realities of life: long periods of life lived together, some meals shared together. A community of goods is sought from the moment that Christians grasp the real meaning of their fraternity.
- These groups demand a liturgical celebration, especially the Eucharist as their right. And they do not rest until they have obtained it. This is a fact that deserves careful study.
- These groups have a tendency to form themselves into an organic and organized body. They create their organs and their offices. We can expect these groups which are more and more numerous to present some

36

of their members for ordination to the diaconate or even the priesthood. As Father Loew has said, religion for them is no longer the obligation to go to Church but the awareness that they themselves are the Church.

• These groups want more decentralization in the Church. They are aware that their existence and their development enhance the success of the ecumenical movement and the march of Christians toward unity.

• These groups want to dialogue with non-Christians and to be as completely open to them as possible.

Therefore, while some structures have difficulty maintaining themselves we must note that life renews itself and develops everywhere. And Christian life spontaneously manifests itself in a community form of life.[4]

Without doubt the parish of the future will be a community of communities. It will group together members of different communities for certain activities, but ordinary life will find its place at the level of the basic community.

Conclusion

This historical survey has been too schematic and we have, without doubt, omitted many points. (It would have been very interesting, for example, to show how all the divisions in the Church have had as their starting point a general weakening of the Christian sense of community.) Our aim has not been to make a historical study but simply to show that what is being done today is deeply rooted in the most authentic tradition of the Church. Despite all the positive things that have just been pointed out, we must admit that throughout the centuries most Christians have been involved in the

37

Church only in certain activities (prayer, meetings, charitable works). This was obviously not something purely negative, but it was involvement in the Church as a society rather than in the Church as a community. It was not a living together — i.e., a sharing at all levels: supernatural, spiritual and material.

The Council ended over 10 years ago and the aggiornamento is still in the early stages of development: It will be able to reach fulfillment only by a return of the Church to its essential form — a community.

CHAPTER 2

THE INTERIOR LIFE OF THE CHRISTIAN COMMUNITY

1. A Community of Faith and Hope

The Community Lives by Faith and Hope

It is faith and hope and the life received in baptism which inserts the Christian into the community. Every Christian has by his baptism, his faith and his hope, a communitarian vocation.

Born of faith in Christ's resurrection and life, as well as in the hope of his return and in the final kingdom, the Christian community can continue to exist in each instant only through faith and hope. A weakening of these virtues necessarily causes deterioration or even the disintegration of the Christian community. The measure of the community's genuineness is the faith and hope of its members. This applies to all aspects of community life: Only faith in the life of the Spirit which animates each of us can make us consider the others as brothers, more brothers than our brothers in the flesh, and can make us stand firm in charity, in oneness of mind and in sharing with them; only faith in the immense communitarian riches of the kingdom of heaven already present can make us accept poverty and the sharing of our possessions; it is only our intentness on the total community promised by Christ that can make us persevere and grow in love, in poverty and in humility.

The Community Is a Living Witness of the Resurrection

Faith in Christ's resurrection is not only belief in a past event, but belief in the life of Christ present today and epitomized in the community. The resurrection of Christ was for the first Christians not only the fact that Jesus was risen but also the fact that this life of Christ appears in the abundant life of the Christian community. The intense life and the extraordinary development of the communities were to their mind the resurrection operating in the body of Christ through the Spirit.

We too have received the Spirit by which Jesus was raised up, but our egotism and selfishness have impeded our openness to the Spirit. Consequently, the Christian community has let itself more or less dissolve. Because we have hindered the Spirit, and often made it impossible for the Spirit to act, we have sometimes smothered our communities by the powerful structures that we have had to contrive in the absence of real communities. Why should we be surprised that we no longer perceive the resurrection and the abundant life of Jesus Christ in these so-called communities? Consequently, our faith in the resurrection of Jesus often becomes a purely intellectual adherence to a historic event of the past, and if we do believe in the life of Jesus in us today this very easily becomes a psychological or even a sentimental matter. And because our community experience does not corroborate the testimony that we have received from the
40

disciples who saw the Risen Jesus, some among us, especially some of the young people, will reject this testimony and will lose the faith.

The Community Is Indispensable

Faith and hope cannot live otherwise than in communities. Faith and hope have a communitarian dimension that has been too much ignored. These "virtues" which come from God are perpetually communicated from one to the other; they maintain themselves in communication, encounter and continual dialogue. For the priest who gives absolution to continue to believe, he needs to realize that the members of his community believe in the absolution that he gives them, and so it is for everything else.

I do not agree with Dietrich Bonhoeffer when he writes: "It is not from within himself that a Christian discovers the capacity to live with other Christians"[5] and when he places the community in the future kingdom. Certainly he *does* say that by a merciful anticipation of the coming kingdom God allows many Christians to live in a community already visible on earth, but he does not sufficiently grasp that the Church is precisely this anticipation. Certainly salvation is entirely gratuitous and grace is not merited, but this gratuitous salvation consists essentially in a summons to an assembly, and the unmerited grace is in itself communitarian. And whoever says "assembly" speaks of a visible unity. Of course, it does sometimes happen that the Christian life can survive and develop in solitude, i.e., without the physical presence of brethren, but then God must provide for this exceptional situation by an exceptional grace.

2. A Community of Love

Love Is Creative

Christians are bound together by the life of the Risen Christ and the Spirit that they have in common. The members of a community communicate life from one to the other. Through each brother, Christ loves the other brethren. Christian love is the likeness of God. But God does not love us because we are just, but he loves us first to make us just. In the same way, it is not first of all the qualities of the brethren which make the brothers love them, but they love them in order to implant these qualities and to save them in Christ.

Jesus has saved us by loving us in the name of his Father. By loving, we in turn heal our brothers spiritually and physically. God hears and answers the prayer of love which we, priests with Christ the Priest, address to him for our brothers and for our sisters. In the community, i.e., in Christ, we thus edify and save one another.

Supernatural love is not simply a beautiful idea, or a splendid sentiment: It includes everything human showing itself in concrete acts and in a continual concern for others. Just in passing let us underline the fact that charity, if it takes root in the very love of Christ, ought to be able to express itself in the characteristics of authentic affection. Let's reject that false spirituality which has taught us to love our brothers without ever daring to show them the affection that the overflowing love of Christ has placed in our hearts. That kind of spirituality has dried up the contacts between members of the same community. Charity needs human gestures, just as much as the soul needs the body.

42

Knowing and Accepting One Another

But love, the force of God in us, the dynamism through which we encounter God, begins with acceptance. All the people the Lord has us meet along the way need to be accepted by us as they are, and not as we would like them to be. They need to feel totally and fully accepted as they are. They need to be sure of never being judged. Everyone has a road to travel, but the plan that God devises for each one to achieve adult stature is probably not the plan that we ourselves would like to make. Therefore, a love which is strong, healing and productive becomes a love which is infinitely respectful. We never know what we are bringing to fruition.

To really achieve mutual acceptance in our communities we must learn to know others and to let ourselves be known by them.

Without knowledge love is impossible. Moreover, it is only by loving that we really know. The members of a community choose, consequently, to reveal themselves in depth to others, so as to be known by them in truth and humility. They do not screen themselves behind a facade, because they are convinced of the need they have for one another. This reciprocal knowledge, which is itself only possible with a great deal of love, enables them to love one another more, to give their lives for one another, to heal one another. Such is the strength of a community.

Loving All the Others

When love is authentic it shines. The love which the brethren have for one another shines out with extraordinary force on all those who are not part of the community. And this love is not that of an isolated individual, himself cut off and whose charity can have little effect. It is a love shared by men who have encountered one another — this encounter has redeemed and divinized their strength to love, it has made their hearts free, rich, inexhaustible, ingenious like that of Jesus Christ.

It is profoundly wrong to think that a real community, by reason of its very fervor, turns in on itself. Those who put forward this objection have never known the life of a real community. When a community turns in on itself it is because its members do not truly love one another.

Indeed, to live a community life means to keep on loving despite the many obstacles, bruises and recurring antipathies. But in this movement it is not possible, so to speak, to stop at the circle of the community. A real community, schooled in love, can never again *refuse* to love those who are not part of it — it is completely oriented towards the problems of others. Real communities, therefore, live in constant concern for their brethren throughout the world. They think particularly of other communities, whether near or far. On the local level, each community must continually renew and readjust itself to the needs of others. Exactly as each community shares its spiritual and material goods within itself, so one community shares with another, even though it be on the other side of the world. An authentic community is a seedbed of universal love and human brotherhood.

We can measure to what degree a decommunitized Church has rendered Christianity inoperative. I remember that during the war, while France was occupied by the Germans, some of us young people asked ourselves an elementary and terrifying question that never seemed to occur to our Christian teachers: "These Germans who have invaded our country are Christians like us — the great majority is baptized and most have kept the faith. What then does brotherhood in Christ mean? Is it not absolute hypocrisy? Without trying to determine who is right and who is wrong the fact is that the common faith and charity of Christians haven't kept them from killing one another. Faith and charity are then illusions and, therefore, they are condemned to disappear." Just an adolescent way of thinking, we say. But the young people spoke the truth. Besides, nothing has changed — we call people whom we crush by our economic system our brothers, and yet the majority of the members of the Holy Catholic Church are underfed and starve to death while the others are stuffed and grow fat.

While we were discussing this one day in July, 1967, in the beautiful Gaspe region of Canada our assembly had the pleasure of hearing a brief and spontaneous statement of a nun who had returned from the Congo. In a word she told us this, "In my parish a group of Christians had formed a Jamaa.[6] Because this Jamaa-community appeared alive and solid, my sisters and I asked to be admitted. We were integrated into this community after being initiated into its life by an older couple. Our Jamaa is our real community and in it we have discovered what it means to be a religious. In our Jamaa live Congolese of three different races. Those who know the Congo know what this means — these people are usually just waiting for the right moment to attack and kill one another. Well, we have gone through everything together and the Jamaa has remained solid and unified because all of us understood that we have the same ancestor, Christ, and that we are really brothers and sisters." The body of Christ is there because love is there.

45

The Third Force

In the world and in the Church today there are two sorts of people — those of the left and those of the right, progressives and reactionaries, socialists and conservatives. Those on the left are for socialism, for a totally renewed and directly accessible liturgy, and for democracy in the Church. Those on the right are for economic and social conservatism, for the preservation of the traditional forms of the liturgy, for authority in the Church.

Far be it from me to consider this situation as shocking or sterile. Ever since man began there have been right-wingers and left-wingers and it even happens sometimes that, because of education and pressures, a sort of compartmentalization takes place which makes a man a leftist in one aspect of life and a rightist in another. This active opposition between conservatism and liberalism is an essential dialectic which is found at the origin of all true human progress. Even Marxists will not disagree with me about this.

However, a point can be reached — and we have reached it — when this active opposition is in danger of rendering us all powerless and of becoming humanly destructive. This point is reached when both liberals and conservatives, disregarding human ties, wish to build reality according to their theories. At that point, liberalism and conservatism have nothing to do with man — they are abstractions. They dominate men rather than serve them and square them off against one another instead of reconciling them in the balanced construction of a growing *body*. Perhaps after the great division caused by the so-called Renaissance and the French Revolution the human "partnership" had to advance in the world and even in the Church by a dialectic of the confrontation of opposites. In any case, it was necessary for genuine socialism to stand against the rule of laissez-faire liberalism, individualism and finance which had established itself. In this way, however, there is an immense danger that one group of men will dominate the other or that society will be mortally paralyzed.

Therefore, quite naturally, we look for a third force. This third force can only be the product of a synthesis — the community is a union of human beings erected on the basis of a principle which is, in short, love.

Love — the most powerful force, the only one able to govern human relations with equality, harmony and unity. Love finds its fulfillment and shows itself in the community. This is why a community is the only place where conservatism and liberalism both find their positive value and join together to build the body. Or better, a community which recognizes neither conservatism nor liberalism but which recognizes men who love one another and who put their diverse outlooks at the service of the whole. And it is rightly love, personal and personalizing love, which shows men the positive and constructive character of their differing outlooks.

Without the community the world appears as nothing more than an inferno of tensions. Without the community the Church itself presents the spectacle of an antagonism that has nothing good or Christian about it (is this not the case in certain countries where conservatives and liberals confront one another?). Without community the Church is burdened by an equally alarming paralysis.

The community is the third force we are looking for everywhere!

A community is not an amorphous whole where each thinks like the other, where all are liberals or else all traditionalists. That would be the ruination of the whole structure. A community has in its midst members with different outlooks, with differently oriented antennas. This is what allows it to be a world, and to be for the world. But these members are members one of the other, they know one another and they love one another. And so by means of a tradition faithfully observed, the whole remains faithful to itself throughout time; and by an openness to the needs of the present it bends without breaking to adapt itself and to serve men.

A community is a place of synthesis. In it the human values and the ground in which they must be rooted are completely preserved. In a community there is no longer left and right, liberal and conservative — all that is surpassed and sublimated in reality.

Because it is a fully human milieu, a community welcomes, as positive and constructive, values which elsewhere are factors of divergence, tension and destruction.

Yes, the community is the third force which many voices call for. It is still perhaps only a humble seed but tomorrow it will be an immense tree under whose branches the multitudes will seek refuge.

3. The Word of God, Prayer and the Sacraments

God, who has spoken to men, who has sent his Word, brings forth the community of salvation. And the Word of God can save only by bringing men together. The history of salvation is the history of this bringing together, worked by the Word. The word of God has been written under the inspiration of the Spirit in the midst of the community of salvation and has been transmitted to us by this very community. It is only by unceasingly receiv-
48

ing this word of God and in responding to it in public and private prayer, in actualizing it in the sacraments today, that the community can continue to exist, repair itself after it has been damaged, remain the light of the world and move towards the ultimate community. I do not have to treat this subject at length because many good things have been written in the last few years which recall these essential truths and show their value. I only want to insist on the fact that without the hearing of God's word, without the sacraments, without public and private prayer, no Christian community is possible. The community comes from above — it is a sheer gift of God.

Without the Word, Prayer and the Sacraments — No Community

Perhaps some communities which appear to be gasping for air have forgotten this somewhat. Perhaps we have been too eager to build a community when a community can only be received from God. Perhaps we have been disappointed in its lack of dynamism when the Spirit is the only dynamism. Perhaps we've gotten ourselves all out of breath running after men, seeking new brethren, when for those who are attentive to his word: "Day by day the Lord added to their community those destined to be saved" (Acts 2:47).

The first step for an assembly which finds itself gasping for air is to return to the scriptures so that the members might receive the word together and find themselves united in the community of salvation. Such a reading should not be a research project of intellectuals but the concern of simple people who have everything to receive, and who are sure that God speaks to them today through the human words and phrases of the bible and that he

49

gathers them together by showing them the path to follow. It is Christ who unites each member to the other and makes them encounter one another, and it is he who gives the community to the world as a light to guide it.

Many communities gasp for air because they no longer receive the word, because their faith in the active word of God has weakened.

If they are attentive to the word of God, the members will be attentive to events in their lives and in the lives of other men. United with Christ, they will see all men and all things as Christ sees them, and their community will progress as the body of Christ grows. They will welcome all men as likenesses of God, all events as divinely intended for their good and therefore they will be involved. . . .

And next we must celebrate the Eucharist, the sacramental act of thanksgiving, not in order to produce a successful liturgy or something that catches on; not in order to sing beautiful hymns or to have the pleasure of saying the Canon in English, but to pray to the Lord together; to offer him thanksgiving together and to let ourselves be joined to the mystery of Jesus, dead and risen. So, in this way we celebrate this liturgy to express and bring into being the true community reunited here and now.

As a result, each member must deepen himself, reach down within himself to that place where he can encounter God and all his brothers and sisters at the same time. This is the only place where egotism is shattered and a genuine community is shaped, a community that never gasps for air but which grows and spreads. And if we live in this way, we will never again gasp for air. For the word of God is sharper than a two-edged sword. The truth cries out in our hearts. Justice and love will show themselves as concrete realities. For the Christian mystery is a mystery of incarnation. The supernatural which does not express itself in earthly realities is a delusion. Love which does not show itself in human acts is hypocrisy. And a community, which is attentive to God's word, cannot tolerate this.

Without the Community — No Word, Prayer, nor Sacraments

We must admit that biblical and liturgical renewal leads to a renewal of community life. This renewal, indeed, leads to a community of shared living and has value only in a community of shared living. If we do not admit this, we frustrate the biblical and liturgical movements. The word of God and the liturgy enable us to live our lives together as children of God. Therefore, if we really do not want to live our common life together in the whole range of our existence, the word of God and the liturgy will become sterile for us. I would say the same thing about a so-called personal encounter with God which would not induce us to encounter our brethren.

We feel ill at ease today. How many Christians really will go along with liturgical reform? This *should* be the expression of a community life and at the same time its source; yet there is no community life or hardly any. The liturgy has become in many cases the support of the spiritual life of individuals and, therefore, the reforms have tried to crack open this mother lode of exclusivity and individualism. This is all very well, but as long as individualism isn't replaced by a community life, Christians will not enter into the mystery of the liturgy and the reforms will miss the mark. It is inevi-

51

table and a good thing that many Christians should find this breach or gap painful.

Some years ago I was distributing communion in a local parish. Suddenly I was struck by something quite ordinary. At the communion rail there were two men— one owned ten houses and was busy buying the eleventh; the other was the father of a large family who never managed to make ends meet. At that moment—just for a second—I seemed to hear a voice cry out "Hypocrite." I found the lie of this so-called "communion" intolerable and I saw myself as one of the crowd in the cafe who can't adhere to a rite, mocked like this by those who still believe. This isn't simplistic—it is the simplicity of the gospel truth. Sacramental communion has no sense if it does not *express* a communion of shared living and does not *lead* to a communion of shared living.

Moreover, the sacramental signs themselves presuppose, as signs, a life-sharing in the Church. The Eucharist has its full sign value in a community where frequent meals shared together are the occasion for giving thanks to the Lord; baptism, in a community genuine enough that the introduction of a new member is not just a formality but a welcoming and acceptance of responsibility for him in the mystery of Christ; penitence, in a community in which the members practice communal sharing, revision of life or the confession of faults made before the Lord[7], the laying on of hands, in an organic community which, feeling the need of diverse offices and seeing members arise in it who are capable of assuming them, delegates them with God and the bishops, for the mission which the Lord gives; marriage, in a community where the members are sufficiently united among themselves and with

52

Christ for the YES of the couple to be the vehicle of their own personal fidelity towards the Lord and towards each other, and for the fruitfulness of the home to be the expression of the spiritual fruitfulness of the love which joins them all. And so on; these examples are not exhaustive. The sacramental sign takes root in the life of the Christian community and we must rediscover this life if we wish to rediscover the value of the sign.

Often the reading of the word of God is done at the level of the community of shared living, for example, in authentic neighborhood communities. If the members permit grace to act in them the results are astounding; these communities become more and more genuine in daily life and they have a perceptible radiance. But the day no doubt will come (it is already on the way) when the sacraments themselves will ordinarily be celebrated in such communities — whether geographical or otherwise — by the ministry of their own priests. The great anonymous assemblies of our cities cannot satisfy the life needs of these communities — not that they are not needed as the manifestation of the large ecclesial community (i.e., a community of communities) but they are not sufficient, and the ordinary liturgical life of Christians cannot be committed to them. Besides, the larger human organizations grow the more men feel the need for small communities of shared living.

Common Prayer

The forms of the eucharistic celebration are being renovated rapidly, the forms of the sacramental celebrations are becoming more accessible. The renewal is not perfect, far from it, because these reforms are not sufficiently derived from the life of authentic communities. Therefore, they still don't show the spontaneity and diversity which are always the signs of life. But at least these reforms *do* exist and they *do* foster an extremely beneficial spirit of inquiry. I would prefer, however, to draw the reader's attention to the problem of common prayer because there is still a great deal that needs to be worked out in this area. Furthermore, note that this problem, in many of its aspects, cuts across the whole question of liturgical reform in general and for this reason I want to spend a little time on it.

The renewal of the Divine Office, first of all, has resulted in a breviary more suited to the actual situation of priests and the active participation of the laity. Permit us to put forward here some reflections which are very dear to us.

It is obvious that for a long time there has been no liturgical prayer outside the Mass and the sacraments for the ordinary communities of Christian people. But, if a Christian community needs to celebrate the Eucharist in its assembly on the Lord's Day and even occasionally during the week, it also has need of morning prayer, of evening prayer and a moment of recollection in the middle of the day, even though all the members cannot participate in every one of these prayer meetings.

Let us even grant that, if absolutely necessary, the priest or priests or the consecrated members of the community, will chant the prayer alone if no other member of the community is free to participate.

But the prayer of the Christian community exists no longer. Of course, in the past there was the breviary that priests said conscientiously, but that office was a monastic office and not an office of the ordinary Christian community. Sunday Vespers and Compline had not been kept up not only because of Latin but also because their liturgical expression didn't correspond to the needs of the Christian people. What we have to find is the prayer of the ordinary Christian community. That is the prayer that the disciples of the Lord, gathered together morning and evening (and even sometimes at noon), will address to God in union with the whole Church. This is the prayer that priests and consecrated members will take up alone when the community cannot meet.

But we know very well that even the new reform of the Divine Office cannot give us what we hope for unless our communities first apply themselves to composing and actualizing their common prayer.

Let it be well understood that we do not want to break with tradition, but on the contrary to rediscover the genuine tradition of the prayer of the Christian people which is extremely simple and which never changes because it is the spontaneous expression of the Spirit in our communities. We listen to God who speaks to us in scripture and, through the commentaries of Christian writers, we sing psalms and hymns, we pray first in silence and then through the intercession of the president of the assembly, and finally we entreat the Lord for the intentions of the Church, of the community, of the world. It is so simple, so spontaneous that, adding to this the celebration of the Eucharist on certain days, we cannot really see how the community could do otherwise. This is the way Christian communities prayed in a time when liturgical expression was alive, with prayers that were spontaneous and original and this is the way we should pray today.

55

In fidelity to this tradition which expresses an internal necessity, we must make a prayer for today's Christian communities. Not for those of the fifth and sixth centuries but for those of today.

To reach this goal there must, first of all, exist a large number of ordinary Christian communities which have been encouraged to find and make known their own liturgical expression. Entrusting themselves to the Spirit, they should be able to show in their prayer what they are today, what their needs are today and what their potentialities are for tomorrow.

Surely, there will be, first of all, readings from the bible, probably a "continuous" reading at the morning office and a reading by "theme" at the evening office. We can never insist too much on the preeminence of God's word. The Lord willed to write down his revelation in human words and phrases for all the ages of the Church. By receiving the immutable word of God, the community keeps its eyes firmly fixed on the ultimate and remains faithful to itself as well as to the Lord's plan for it and for the world. It is just too bad if the language of the bible seems difficult and archaic to us—it is up to us to accustom ourselves to it, to form ourselves through contact with it, conscious of the great treasure that God has given us.

And when we have heard the word, we will meditate on it by singing inspired psalms. We will know how to make a suitable choice. We will know how to use only some parts of a psalm or how to compose a hymn by joining together verses on the same theme from different psalms. We will also know how to sing these biblical hymns.

But there will be not only biblical readings and psalms. At the morning office, there are readings of texts from the Fathers and Doctors of the Church. Among these texts there are some that are interesting and nourishing, there are others that mean less to us. Why defer to authors of the fifth or sixth century? According to the most venerable tradition, we do not read their works in our liturgical assemblies because they are Fathers or Doctors but, on the contrary, they are called Doctors and Fathers because we read their works in liturgical assemblies. Let's go back to this sound tradition.

Have we no genuine Fathers and Doctors of the Church in the 20th century? We don't dare cite them because they are really too numerous. . . . What keeps us from reading their best pages, or certain passages from an encyclical in our communities? Don't we have today, in some books that have appeared recently, homilies which are better and more true for our age than those of a St. Augustine? After all the Holy Spirit isn't dead! But until now the reforms have been carried out as if we refused to believe that the Holy Spirit can still inspire today. Genuine tradition has been and must always be innovating. The liturgical tradition of the Church is the word of God and the sacraments whose essential rites were founded by Christ. We must remain faithful to this and remain faithful to the spontaneous forms in which the wisdom of the Spirit has cast the Church's prayer. But this tradition cannot be allowed to paralyze us. There is a fidelity which pretends to be faithful to tradition but which is contrary to genuine tradition and to the Spirit who has always guided it.

What can we say about liturgical singing? We have never kept strictly to the psalms. It is normal for the Christian community to express its faith, hope and love in hymns it has composed. We note, in Paul's letters and

57

in the First Letter of Peter, traces of important early Christian hymns and even one or two in their entirety. Each age of the Church has composed its own hymns—though during the period of liturgical sclerosis we were afraid to introduce them into the "official" prayer.

The curious thing is that Christian liturgical and artistic creativity flourished in those periods of history which were the most authentically communitarian. Liturgical creativity and also poetic and musical creativity of the Christian Church are not primarily the work of great men, but of communities. They are the expression of a community. The lack of liturgical and artistic expression in the Church proves beyond doubt a lack of communitarian life. We can confirm this assertion with many proofs. For example, we have bestowed a somewhat impoverished and socially fragmented Western Christianity on the Bantus of Africa which in no way corresponds to their communitarian inclinations. We have not tried to animate their existing communities by the Holy Spirit, we have not given them the added spiritual impulse that their communities expect from the Church and which they need so badly. This is the reason for such extremely poor artistic expression, which is all the poorer because the rigid Roman liturgy was imposed on these peoples and did not correspond at all to their mentality. The Bantus were not allowed to make a liturgy. We have finally opened our eyes—a little late. If we leave the Jamaa and the new black monasteries alone we will see an authentic African religious expression come to life. We should note that the American negroes encountered Christianity in a form which showed more respect for their communities and which even vivified them. From these communities came the incomparable negro spirituals whose influence on music

58

has been considerable and which are the authentic evidence of a young faith nourished by ancestral images.

Let's live in the Christian community of the last half of the 20th century and this community will create poetry, music, architecture capable of expressing the prayer of the late 20th-century Christians. Spontaneously and inevitably, the new forms of prayer will find their proper place in the assembly gathered together for the liturgy. We must make up our minds about this. We shouldn't be holding onto the pipe organ with all our strength in this age of electronic music.

We have talked about readings from the bible, readings from the Fathers and Doctors, some psalms, some songs and hymns. Let us emphasize silent prayer and the need to prolong it. At its peak the unanimity of spirits and hearts before God is best expressed by silence. We must rediscover silence, a silence full of our unity before the grandeur, mercy and salvation of God. Silence is the most beautiful music. This is the eternal music to which God calls us.

Then there is the prayer of the president of the assembly which sums up the prayer which is in everyone's heart. Our Roman prayers used to be very beautiful. Unfortunately, they don't always correspond to our way of thinking and speaking. Isn't it time to construct new ones? The Council has opened up new paths never thought of by the Fathers and it is normal for this new theology, this new way of understanding God's message, to manifest itself in the solemn prayers of the president. The alteration of some of the prayers in the liturgy shows that the Church has already understood this. But aside from this, much work still remains to be done. And the real work will come spontaneously at the grass-roots level, from the prayer of living communities.

59

We offer these few reflections to the consideration of the Christian communities and ask that they themselves try to invent prayer. Without pretension, but with conviction, we offer them as well to all those whose mission it is to promote and authenticate the renewal of the prayer of the Church.

The Real Sense of the Sacred

Now and then certain people seem to fear that the sense of the sacred, with which it seems the Christian cult must be surrounded, will be harmed by a community life which expresses itself in an overly familiar and spontaneous liturgy. This fear shows a dangerously materialistic conception of Christianity.

Some time ago Father Sainsaulieu wrote in a weekly magazine:

"Before God revealed himself, the sacred was the divine. It related us to an unknown God. It is not then an idea from the gospel but rather ballast taken on when the yacht became a tramp steamer.

"It is grossly ridiculous to make it a test of authentic Christianity. The bitter experience of the 18th and 19th centuries, which emphasized the sacred even more than the Middle Ages, is not far off. The French stopped moving forward—they rejected all belief. But the 20th century has flowed in the opposite direction and people of all ages have again found their way to God.

"Too much emphasis on the sacred keeps us from drawing near to God in our daily life. Does the heart of Jesus really need a throne? The whole gospel answers, 'no.' It is the history of religion which, like a good pagan, has seen the sacred everywhere and reduced the religious to the sacred. It is easier than talking of love and holiness.

60

"In the Eucharist, the bread, the wine and the table are not there to scare us. They are the measures taken by Jesus on the eve of his death against the sacralization of love. That is the touchstone, the heart of Christianity.

"Let us render to Caesar his fears and to Christ his revolution. Was he not killed so as to overturn the barriers between men and God?"

Genuine Christian sacredness is not where we have often presumed it to be. The Father is adored in spirit and truth and the presence of Christ is revealed today in a community where two or three are gathered together in his name, where the bread of his body is broken and where the cup of his blood is drunk in memory of him. Our contemporaries have fled from our incense smoke and our splendid processions. They have refuted the glittering spectacle of ecclesiastical pomp. They no longer believe in a grand display in the service of God. They disown the Constantinian basilica and the worldly ostentation of the imperial court which hides and distorts the simple liturgy of the fraternal assembly which met at Cecilia's house.

In Jesus, God committed himself to man. He was born in a manger. After 30 he became a man always on the move, he celebrated the Last Supper on a table among the Twelve, he died on the cross. Our Christian Churches have nothing to do with the temple in Jerusalem or with Mt. Garizim. The sacred is in the spirit and in truth, it is in the love which unites the brethren around their Lord. In this alone will modern man unite with us and go with us to the Father.

We understand the parishes in Panama City or Oklahoma which were born and live without buildings and which bring together real communities where the sacred liturgy is celebrated, without show, in the familiar setting of the fraternal reunion and celebrated as an integral and dynamic part of the common life.

4. The Community of Goods

If any subject is hard to discuss and likely to shock it is the community of goods. We want a Christianity which is pious, apostolic and charitable but we don't want to even hear talk about Christianity thrusting itself into material realities and producing a social order based on sharing. It is too compromising. And, besides, this might bring back the detested Middle Ages. We must free our minds on this subject and perhaps the best way to start is by looking boldly at the history of the first centuries of the Church.

The Church of the first three centuries voluntarily practiced a community of goods. Father Rene Carpentier, S.J., and a team of young Jesuits at Louvain have applied themselves for ten years now to studying all the Christian texts of the first centuries in an effort to reveal the life of some communities, particularly in regard to the pooling of material possessions. The consequence of this study was a series of master's theses. We cannot thank the authors too much for the important work they have accomplished. It is not my intention to hand on the results of their inquiry but I would like to try to show the mentality of those Christian communities which are face to face with the problem of material possessions, by dwelling on some characteristic texts.

You are familiar with the two passages from the Acts of the Apostles describing the life of the Jerusalem community (cf. Acts 2: 42-47; 4: 32-35). The problem is to determine whether these two pericopes are exceptions, a few meteors passing through the sky of history, or whether they are two examples among others of the ordinary catechesis and general practice of the Christian Churches of the first centuries.

Father Carpentier says that according to the studies we mentioned: "The *koinonia* formed part of the ordinary catechesis of all the faithful. In the documents we are dealing with, it was the normal practice and was not the exception." The teaching and practice of a community of goods is so closely linked to the ordinary Christian life that when the texts don't mention it, it is because the matter is so evident and well known. We seldom bother to write down everyday things.

I offer only a few texts for your consideration.

In Second Corinthians, Paul mentions the collection that he is making for the Church in Jerusalem. What he asks for, what he seeks, is an "equalization" of the material condition of the Christians of Corinth and those of Jerusalem:

> This does not mean that to give relief to others you ought to make things difficult for yourselves: It is a question of balancing what happens to be your surplus now against their present need, and one day they may have something to spare that will supply your own need. That is how we strike a balance: as scripture says: *The man who gathered much had none too much, the man who gathered little did not go short.* (2 Cor. 8: 13-15).

The Didache (an Eastern work of the end of the first century):

> You will not push aside the indigent but you will share everything mutually with your brother and you will not say that something belongs to you alone. If

you share immortal goods together how much more should you share perishable goods!

Letter to Diogentes (end of the 2nd century):

They all share the same table.

Tertullian (in Africa towards 200) speaking to pagans said:

We do not think of goods as private. While in your case your inherited wealth makes all brotherhood impossible, in our case it is by our inherited wealth that we become brothers. . . . We who are in communion in heart and spirit do not hold anything back from the communion of goods. Everything among us is in common, except marriage.

St. Cyprian (Africa, about 230):

Today we do not give even half of our inherited wealth although the Lord commanded us to sell it. But let us at least give the profits.

St. Irenaeus (Lyons, about 200):

Jews give a tenth of their goods to God; Christians give everything they have (and not just a little part) for the use of the Lord (that is to the Church for the poor), giving freely and with joy because they hope for goods of a higher order.

The Latin author Lucian wrote:

Christians despise all possessions and share them mutually.

St. Thomas (13th century):

Sin has made the division of goods necessary but they ought to be for the common use.[8]

64

These texts prove to us that the primitive Church lived in an authentic community of goods. This is irrefutable. Some gave everything they owned to the Church, but this was not obligatory. However, it is clear that the sum of each one's goods (whether it be inheritance, profit or salary) was considered as belonging to Christ. The Christian is no longer an owner but only a responsible manager.

Because everything belongs to Christ, no individual is able to use what he possesses (even if he earned it by hard work) without taking into consideration the needs of all his brothers and sisters: first of all, his wife and children who are his closest brethren, then the brothers and sisters of his small community, then those of other communities. And there must be, as St. Paul said, "equality."

Such is the simple and traditional teaching of the first Christian centuries. This is what inspired St. Thomas and it is this which will finally determine the outcome of the position the Church has recently taken toward the sharing of mutual goods and the community of use.

The brotherhood of all in Christ is the starting point for the community of goods. Because Christians have one heart and one soul they are truly brothers and consequently they share what they have.

It is not a matter then of a new law but of love which shows itself in life concretely. We find many indications in the texts of the total surrender of wealth but this was not obligatory. There are no allusions to taxes or percentages. Nor do we find any seeking of poverty for its own sake.

What does oblige everyone and applies to everything is the need to share. This is the indispensable expression of love. Everything belongs to God, and the Christian

65

who has possessions has the mission to love others in the name of God by passing his blessings on to them. In this way a new social order which is light-years away from the juridical laws now in force is instituted. . . . It is a matter of a free and voluntary sharing, affecting the use of all goods. Certainly this community of goods will appear in diverse forms according to circumstances and it will vary according to the degree of faith and the hope of Christians, but it will always appear as the indispensable sign of divine love and brotherhood in Christ. Persecutions will favor this sharing of possessions (just as it favors other aspects of the evangelical life) but will never bring it into being.

Are we dealing with the new social order? We must answer, yes. According to Tertullian, there is radical opposition between the viewpoint of Christians on the use of goods and that accepted by the surrounding society. And, according to St. Irenaeus, while Jews give a tenth of their earnings and are able to use the rest themselves, Christians reserve everything to the use of the Lord. Among them, then, it is not a matter of a tax (which would be a juridical measure) but of the other directedness of all goods. Here is how Father Rene Carpentier puts it:

"Do we have here a different system of possessions? Or only a commendable disposition which applies solely to that part of our goods that we determine superfluous while the rest, the mass of our wealth, capital and profit, is considered, pure and simple, our property and our absolute right?

"All the texts of the early communities indicate that the gospel message introduced a new concept which applied to all goods. They have an owner who is consequently responsible for them but they are intended for

66

the use of all. . . .

"If there are really two systems for the use of goods, we can understand how it came to be that Christians, who had increased in numbers and had been freed from persecution, became unfortunately involved in the juridical order of pagan society. The fervent members of the *koinonia* could not reconcile themselves to this and felt themselves strongly drawn to create a new community, a real *koinonia* in the desert.

"A new phase of history began when the Christian system joined hands with Roman law and then with the traditional law of the invading peoples to establish a society which was more and more exclusively composed of Christians.

"We cannot deal with this complex evolution which was the result of the encounter and collaboration of these three currents.

"Christianity deeply marked the whole of civilization, thanks especially to monasticism. And in this way, the community spirit was never completely absent from the history of the Middle Ages, and it existed right up to the French Revolution. We can provide many proofs of it.

"But the juridical attitude became more influential and even became predominant because of the intervention of the 'legists,' the interests of princes, and the multiplication of nations, and because of the increase of wealth and the power of money, commerce, banks, etc.

"The Church opposed loans made at interest for so long because it was conscious of this evolution towards an external juridical order where legalism would overwhelm personal values.[9] It was accepted only when, in popular opinion, money had become a value, a claim in itself. Because of 'extrinsic titles,' as the Church continued to say, money was able then to make us completely forget its relation to a personal value."[10]

We cannot help thinking that the Church partly bungled its opening to the world when, giving up its efforts to impregnate the world with its principles, it accepted the Roman juridical order, blended into civil society and accepted the triumph of law to the detriment of personal values (even within itself). Consequently, the Church has not sufficiently been the salt, light or leaven of the world.

The Community of Goods Today

Justification

Before opening the discussion of the "justification" of the community of goods today, I offer for your consideration these simple words of Dominique Chenu:

"A similar religion (that of the Promise) evidently denounces at great cost to itself the behavior which leads men to express their divinization only in their souls without involving the substance of their daily existence. The Promise would be ridiculous if, while projecting its fulfillment into an eternal beyond, it did not progressively incarnate itself into time, into the contents and elements of time starting with its basic economic condition. The religion of the Promise unceasingly denounces the false spiritualism of a devotion and a cult which would exile man from his possessions and his earthly needs. At the extreme, superstition which dehumanizes because it disincarnates the Promise, puts it outside of history which is meant to bring it to fulfillment. The Gospel describes itself as yeast which lifts up all the dough, and the first rising is an economic life which provides for the production of goods and the just satisfaction of the needs of all. Brotherhood starts there and puts to the test, right away, our fidelity to the word of God."[11]

Let us first recall some principles at the risk of partially repeating ourselves. Christ has taken hold of us to make us one body. Along with our persons he has taken hold of our possessions which are the indispensable extension of ourselves. Therefore, all that we possess belongs ultimately to Christ. We are only the managers — but trustworthy and responsible managers. Because everything belongs to Christ we cannot use the goods which we manage without considering the needs of the whole body, i.e., our brethren, starting with those closest to us.

Our union in Jesus by the one Spirit that the Father has infused into our souls is primary. But we are not dealing here with only a spiritual union but a complete union which implies a community of goods. Therefore, the community of goods is one of the normal and indispensable expressions of our union in Christ.

It comes from an internal need and is not imposed by law. But it is certainly an important criterion by which we can discern whether or not we are dealing with a real community. It is an indispensable sign of communitarian life and it forcibly helps the communitarian life to maintain itself and continue — it is a sort of sacrament of our authentic brotherhood in Christ. We can understand Tertullian when he said "it is by our inherited wealth that we become brothers."

Certainly the community of goods can be realized in different ways. It can be accomplished through a community in the strict sense of the word (religious communities and some lay communities) where all the goods become collective property administered by the community as such or by elected superiors. Or the community of goods may be brought about through a simple

69

sharing, with each one keeping the ownership of his goods but with a frank openness to others and with a concern for the needs of all. There is a whole range of possibilities between these two styles of Christian collectivism but, in fact, in the theocentric and Christocentric view of the world, the community of goods and the sharing of possessions both have the same meaning — the forms may vary but the reality is the same.

It is important to highlight the eschatological character of the community of goods once more. Because we will share immortal goods we also share perishable goods (of Didache). As the rule of my community puts it: "The community of goods is imposed in one way or another on all those who are conscious of walking together towards the communitarian Good par excellence: the Kingdom of Heaven." The community of goods is an exterior and visible anticipation of the kingdom of heaven already present in us. It anticipates the reality to come and expresses in a tangible way the reality already present in our hearts.

What is the kingdom of heaven already present and still to come if it is not our total unity in Christ, the unity to which all men are summoned with us? Why do men work, why do they use material things? What is the ultimate end of all their efforts, what is it they want to express, announce or achieve? It is the perfect unity, openness and the fusion of their beings. Whether men know it or not, the essential value of material things is that they are the vehicle of unity. Their purpose is to help men to fulfill their interior unity and to attain the fullness of Christ. Christians have the mission to experience and actively express the unifying goal of material goods. They should then make these things a concrete factor of unity among themselves and with all men,

70

making use of these material things to consolidate human brotherhood.

The *Constitution on The Church in the Modern World* (no. 70) as well as the encyclical *Populorum Progressio* (nos. 22, 23, 24) reminds us that the goods of the earth are for common use and that there are limits to the right of private ownership. If we don't want the truths of these documents to remain sterile knowledge, we must build the foundation of human society on the basis of groups in which the common purpose of goods will be approved and concretely realized. If the regime of sharing and the economy of need do not first exist in the "basic communities," they will never exist on the national or worldwide levels. The new economy required to save mankind today demands such a change of mentality, such a transcending of egotism that it must necessarily restructure itself at the grass-roots level where moral values can most immediately operate and become concrete. This is the reason for the principal importance of communitarian achievements even though they are still humble and small — they carry the humanity of tomorrow within themselves.

Certainly the Christian community, inasmuch as it is the Church, does not need to concern itself with achieving a community of the means of production. It is not the Church's role to cultivate the earth or to make cheese or toys. It may happen that a Christian community does these things, but not as the Church, and to avoid any confusion it is better in this case that this community of production be established on a larger base with some non-Christians. What is primarily asked of Christians is that they pool together or share in the use of their consumer goods. If Christians live in this way, the influence of their example and their spirit will hasten

71

the communalization of the means of production which is so often needed. Today we hear the objection that the state sees to a certain equality in material standards through its taxes and social laws, etc. This objection is not without foundation. But we must say that it is far from correct, so much the more because this embryo of social equality is in fact achieved at the price of the impoverishment of the poor nations.

Equality will never exist in a society based on laws. For equality to exist, the soul stands in need of an additional something — it needs love. That's why the Church, which claims to be the witness of God's love for all his children, has to speak out.

Another objection to the principle of material equality exists in the very small number of *real* communities. This is a serious objection. But it is useless to be encumbered by our past individualism, and it is always wrong to look at the present without perceiving in it the currents which will determine the future. The fact is that some communities do exist — and more and more of them. The fact is that within these communities men are seeking an authentic sharing of material goods. These communities must seek out one another and join together; because while a community isn't very much in isolation, it is something and it *can* be a great deal once it is joined to others. A community of communities, especially if these have different material opportunities and different resources (for example, if we are dealing with communities from economically developed countries and from underdeveloped countries) is a leaven whose possibilities for enlightening and transforming the milieu go far beyond the number of individuals involved.

Realizations

The *Courrier Communautaire International* conducted a small survey on the community of goods in 1967. I do not intend to list the results here. As soon as a community is formed, that is, as soon as the members really become brothers and sisters, the problem of sharing things presents itself. How could it be otherwise? Each of the studies published by the *Courrier Communautaire International* insists that the union of persons, of spirits and hearts, precedes and conditions the community of possessions. This must never be forgotten. But once there is a real union of persons, the problem of the sharing of possessions is inevitably posed.

Let us see, for example, how the community groups founded by Father Varillon, S.J., looked at the question:

"Money is the testing ground of our basic attitudes — there is no deed involving fairness which does not make us face the test of money at certain moments. There is no authentic charity which doesn't oblige us to surrender a portion of our goods; no Eucharistic Sacrifice which does not lead us to consider money's relativity and give us the strength to go beyond it.

"On the other hand, the way we handle our money can be a good means of educating our deepest spiritual attitudes. On a subject so difficult to grapple with, a community group can be a support and an irreplaceable teacher. Indeed, in our century a very heavy taboo forbids any discussion of money — a sort of deplorable shame keeps us from discussing a key element which is related to justice in our lives and in our institutions and which also is related to love.

"Relinquishing the ownership mentality, to switch from looking at material goods as things to be owned to looking at them as things to be managed, is not only

73

a matter of good will, nor is it a matter even of determination. It's the result of a long education which dethrones the subject's passion for ownership. It is also the result of progressive training on a few points. We cannot then conveniently have a common norm for all the community groups. Each of them, therefore, decides once a year the forms they intend to use to carry out this education and training. We are in an area where the imagination can run free and so these can take quite different forms. Let us cite some ways of operating which neither limit nor exclude one another:

"—there may be consideration of the use of the money of a household or of a celibate or widowed member; or two couples might explain their expenses in front of a third couple so that all three can ponder them;

"—there may be a consideration of income, its sources, the conditions in which money is earned;

"—there may be an attempt at equal distribution, with each one saying what sum he will contribute to the common fund or what sum he requests from this fund, or even that he will neither contribute nor ask anything. Obviously the purpose for which the funds may be used must be spelled out;

"—there may be a more total equalization among some members who are ready for this experience, or a quite different form combining or completing these few examples.

"The truth is that these limited and tentative efforts are the first steps on a road whose destination cannot be known in advance."

A spirit of resoluteness and prudence marks this text. We can see this. It isn't easy to go forward in this area when our whole western juridical system goes against it. And yet the juridical system itself will not evolve unless many groups seek to advance. . . .

In such a community families and single members have been willing to let one another know their financial situation. In this way, then, when one of them is in difficulty, the others can give him what he needs to extricate himself — this is what is called "the principle of communicating vessels." And those who give feel that they are giving nothing because they are only managers. This brother has a right to what they give because he is their brother and so, strictly speaking, they don't give him anything. Obviously this presupposes a gradual formation and an awareness of the fullness of Christian reality.

In other communities a common fund is created which is always empty because it is shared with brethren in poor countries. To establish this common fund, each contributed in proportion to his standard of living. A great deal of openness, one to the other, was needed for this. They understood that this one needs a car for the traveling that his work requires, that someone else must entertain a great deal, etc. Once those "professional" expenses were deducted, they allocated a common amount such that the living standard of each person was similar. It was not easy.

The Focolari have a strict community of goods for their consecrated members (single people and some families), while the "enlisted" families which form cells of volunteers give their surplus to the group. The African Brotherhoods have a very flexible system which leaves a great deal of freedom to the families but which, considering the poor conditions, leads to an extensive degree of financial solidarity. Many "Equipes Notre-Dame" in France and Belgium are trying to pool their goods but at this moment I am not able to give other details. And so we could go on and on.

In the city of Brussels alone there are many communities, two of which, grouping families and single people, have achieved a particularly full community of goods (common funds) while leaving to families the whole responsibility for the amount allocated to them by the community. There are similar examples in all the countries of the world.

I would like to cite here two reports — one comes from a parish in a large city where they had posed the problem of the sharing of goods; the other describes my personal experience of living for some years now in my own community.

Here then is how a parish recently stated the problem of the communion and sharing of goods:

"First of all, if we no longer succeed in living like the Christians of the first centuries, it is because we don't really love one another. We don't have one heart and one soul. We don't even know one another. The parish is composed of different groups — one group doesn't know the other and the mutual knowledge and love which are essential for the Christian life are not found within each group. Consequently, a community of goods is unthinkable for us. We cannot share — all we have left is the ability to 'do charity.' We need to educate ourselves. We must try in each group to know and love one another better. We must create ties between the members of different groups. We must humanize the parish machinery. The divine cannot function without the human.

"The members of each group must also teach one another to rethink the use of earthly goods. Each one, personally and with his family, has to learn anew that he is not an owner but a manager, and that he cannot use

76

what he possesses without considering the needs of his brothers and sisters. We are then asked to work on ourselves while supported by fraternal dialogue.

"Having said this we have to recognize that civil society today is trying to restore to its citizens a certain equality of living standards. Capitalism is far from dead, but in this technological world we are moving little by little towards a one-class society. Certainly this will always be far from perfect both because of man's egotism and because the social movement, which is already developing among us, develops at the expense of the Third World. That's why it is high time that we rediscovered the genuine Christian point of view on material goods. Otherwise, once the problem of a country such as Latin America is settled, another similar problem, perhaps more dreadful, will crop up elsewhere. We have to realize that civil society has established a certain degree of equality among us that didn't exist 50 years ago, but that this equilibrium must extend to the ends of the earth. And for that to happen, we will have to change ourselves.

"Another consideration: We are still a little ashamed to talk about money to one another. The examples that have been given in the *Courrier Communautaire International* still seem inaccessible to us, at least for the moment. We are not open enough with one another. We don't really step out of our individualism. Unless we become involved in sharing with brethren who are in real need we will never step out of our individualism, we will never share with one another.

"For some years we have supported a parish in Jordan. In reality this twin parish doesn't interest us because we don't know it. We ought to be working hand in hand but no, all we do is give them an offering

77

every year. We do indeed announce a collection from the pulpit and in the parish bulletin but that involves only a donation and doesn't lead to sharing. But sharing is what must take place. And sharing means mutual knowledge and love.

"Here is what we propose: That the parish count on the members of each group to make an effort towards better mutual knowledge which will motivate us to share with our sister-parish. The members of each group will discuss together the question of the material help that they can contribute to it, and in this way each group will be able to determine what it can allot to the sister-parish annually, and later perhaps monthly. And to determine what they can allot they will try little by little to get rid of the taboo about money so as to be able to reveal their own financial situation to one another and come to the point of forming an equitable common fund.

"In this way the fraternal help we will offer will be the beginning of a real sharing with our brothers in need, and this love of others will have made us encounter one another in our own groups and in our parish.

"We must then establish more personal contacts between the parish in Jordan and ourselves. A visit by our pastor and our curate would give us information about the needs of our Arab brothers. We must increase these contacts. Isn't it possible that some of the young people of this parish will someday journey to help our brothers to reach a higher stage of development . . . ?

"But because sharing isn't real as long as it's unilateral, when we know our brothers better we will ask them to share their spiritual and cultural riches with us and we will learn to know them so that our hearts may be as big as the world!"

And here is the history of my little community on the

question of material goods.

At the very beginning we chose the community pooling of goods instead of sharing. However, we didn't succeed overnight in making the community what it is today. There have been two major phases and we are still moving forward.

Phase one: The community pooling of goods was considered as total spiritually, but it was carried out in a very flexible way. Each month every family put the amount, at which it had arrived in private with the priest, into the common fund. The priest took into account the family's financial situation, its social responsibility and the number of children. This amount varied according to circumstances but never without the agreement of the priest. To achieve this pooling each had to deprive himself of a bit of luxury.

As you can see, the members of the community at first left it to the priest to decide with each of them what they should contribute to the common fund. They trusted in his judgment and in this way they maintained a certain secrecy between one family and another, between one member and another.

One of the brethren was put in charge of the common fund and he kept the community regularly informed of its development. Once the expense of providing a house for the community (where they spent every second Sunday together, met each Tuesday evening and where a "displaced person" could live, partly supported by the community) and the cost of the days of common life, of apostolic work were covered, what was left was given to those in need, to charitable works, etc. The brethren used the major part of their salary which was left to them with a certain measure of control from the priest and

79

the community. Every two months each family presented its accounts to the priest. The priest kept his eye on current expenses to see that everyone kept within the limits of a well-defined Christian poverty. When it was a question of unusual and important expenditures, the community came together to discuss them: Eventually the common fund would help each brother to make the important expenditure that he had decided upon.

Let us add that juridically nothing changed. He who owned his house still had it as far as the law was concerned. Even if each was dispossessed spiritually, only income from all sources was actually involved.

As you can see, the system was too complicated and too paternalistic (even though everyone had worked it out and wanted it). It was a stage. The experiment wasn't sufficiently conclusive because the priest was forced to consider, in the pooling together, the different members' degree of communitarian conviction and this made it less authentic. Finally, if the method did form the spirit of poverty, if it did breed a real fraternal spirit, it was not communitarian enough in itself. After a difficult crisis, we were able with the Lord's help to change to a method both simpler and more radical.

Phase two: Salaries, income, family allowances were put into the common fund. This was managed by the community who appointed someone to be responsible for all the material aspects of its life and a treasurer who kept the funds and the books.

For the remainder, every month each family and each single person receives a sum which covers his food, clothing, relaxation, heat, light, travel and school costs. A scale has been set which determines the amount allocated to married persons, to single people and to
80

children according to their age. The scale is applied flexibly because the governing principle is to give to each according to his needs. When the needs of some family go beyond the fixed scale, they are not afraid to say so and since we love them enough to accept them as different they receive more according to the possibilities of the common fund: On the other hand when returns have not been sufficient or when some expenses are too high (at the moment we are repairing two houses) we all accept a cut in pay.

It is agreed that each family and each single person should dispose of the sum given him every week as he likes. So, for example, the mothers of our families, like those everywhere, manage their budget to suit the needs of their husbands and their children — they save to buy clothing, etc.

Civil law does not recognize the community, so that juridically the houses remain the property of the individual. We have, nonetheless, considered buying a building as joint owners, but we want to move slowly and prudently in this matter.

Phase three: Four members of a community of women which grew out of our little community have gone to Ruanda. Our sisters work with two priests in a new parish where they try to live as communally as possible with the natives. We want to reach the point of forming more than spiritual and moral bonds between our community and this newborn community in Ruanda. We want to reach the point where the two communities will be joined on the economic level. In fact, this already partly exists but we want to tear down the walls between the developed and "underdeveloped" to more concretely achieve a community of communities.

Well, there it is, although everything hasn't been said and lots of problems doubtlessly have been left hanging. But the community *does* exist and *does* live and this truth is the basis of all our hopes.

Vatican II and the Community

We are sometimes asked if the problem of the community was examined by the Second Vatican Council. Certainly the conciliar documents often use the word "community" but in a very vague way it would seem, and not in the precise sense that we understand it. Exception must be made, of course, for number 15 of the *Decree on the Renewal of the Religious Life* and the many words of encouragement which introduce some observation for the lives of priests (*Decree on the Pastoral Office of Bishops,* art. 30, no. 1; *Decree on the Ministry and Life of Priests,* arts. 8 and 17). As you can see, when the Council spoke of communities in the strict sense of the term, it was dealing with religious or priests. This limited reference shouldn't surprise us — the ordinary Christian community which came into existence 2,000 years ago has undergone numerous changes and no longer has the appeal to hold the attention of most of the Church, or of the world. Let us face it — the ordinary Christian community needs to be reborn.

Nevertheless, it wouldn't be quite right to think that the Christian community, in the strict sense, was without its defenders and promoters at the Council.

Let us recall the intervention of Bishop Elchinger on October 18, 1963:

Do we all agree that the major heresy of our age, a real pastoral heresy, is the individualism that is everywhere, including in the Church, and that Vatican II should do something to cure it? Let us give dogmatic value to the Church as a community. Let's form small communities of Christians like those of the first days so that we may rekindle the world. . . .

But we are pleased to be able to put forward another text. I am referring to the speech Bishop Himmer of Tournai presented to the Council's office at the beginning of November, 1964. This amendment was signed by 24 bishops. You recall that the text of the famous Schema 13 was discussed during the third session from October 20 to November 10, 1964, and that because of the lack of time many of the last speeches were only submitted to the office instead of being given orally before the assembly. This was the fate of the following document and the reason why the press failed to mention it. Except for one phrase the Constitution *Gaudium et Spes* on *The Church in the Modern World* paid no attention to the proposed amendment. This is certainly to be regretted. We can, however, be pleased that such a large number of bishops thought it good to countersign it once they heard of the document. Isn't it encouraging for us that this document was a conformity pledge to the gospel and to the Spirit of Christ?

Everything in the text isn't equally pleasing. There is a certain timidity evident about a more generalized call to a communitarian life. This is explained by the fact that the community pooling of goods is considered far too strictly, at the same time failing to work out the theology of ownership and to distinguish between juridical ownership and use. But, on the other hand, some things are excellent. Note for example (no. 2) how the text places the maxim "from each according to his capacities to each according to his needs" in the perspective of the gospel and makes it, we might say, the economic expression of an authentic brotherhood in Christ. Note also that it was of foremost importance to the authors that communities serve as a demonstration of the Church's doctrine that material goods are for the benefit of all.

Here is the text:
"We would like the 'forms and institutions by which the appropriation, production and distribution of the goods of the earth are achieved to be unceasingly adapted prudently and firmly in accord with their final end, namely the benefit of all men.'[12] These rather vague words seem to contain an invitation to look for more concrete forms and to bring them into being. We might be allowed, then, to say a word about the form of life which is called 'communitarian.' 1. Let us remember first of all that the Church has traditionally gladly encouraged communities created under the guidance of the evangelical spirit. Refer to the Acts of the Apostles where the first Christian assemblies are described. Thus in chapter 2:44: 'The faithful all lived together and owned everything in common; they sold their goods and possessions and shared out the proceeds among themselves according to what each one needed.' Likewise in chapter 4:32: 'The whole group of believers was united, heart and soul; no one claimed for his own use anything that he had, as everything they owned was held in common.' Afterwards there were the communities of monks and the familial communities (often the two were associated) which were greatly responsible for the construction of Europe.

"2. Even today we still find Christians and not only religious but also laymen (married and single) who,
84

driven by the same inspiration, have established and live in similar communities, while still others are thinking about setting them up. Well then, these communities must be thought about: Their members are joined together in such a way their material goods are common property: Each contributes to the community according to his own ability and each receives according to his needs. As is clearly evident, these communities of Christians are based on the principle of religious and Christian order, namely, that their fraternal union in Christ and in the Church should lead them to a common sharing of goods not only of spiritual but even of material goods.

"3. This initiative of some Christians also constitutes a return to a more natural common utilization of goods like that which is still practiced quite widely in African civilization and other places where, in the same way, the end sought out is not profit but satisfaction of the needs of each individual. It might be said in passing that if the Church would pay more attention to these matters she would understand the forms of life and the institutions of these people more easily, and consequently also have more effective access to them.

"4. Even if we can forsee that there won't be many forms of this common life, this is no reason for rejecting them, on the contrary, they need to be sustained. Indeed, in a world like ours which is too often dominated by the hard law of profit and also by the international dictatorship of money (cf. *Mater et Magistra*), the example of these communities is of very great importance because it inclines their fellow citizens to change their style of life, which is one founded on the law of profit, and to soften the pernicious effects of such a law.

"5. In addition, it can be seen that this communitarian form of life cannot generally persevere in fidelity

85

to its initial resolution without the help of divine grace and the strength of the Holy Spirit, especially in today's atmosphere which broils with the frenzied desire for personal profit. Consequently, these communities will be signs: Through them the Church's doctrine that material goods are for the benefit of all will be demonstrated more clearly and in this way the Church herself will become more concretely the light of nations.

"I suggest that on p. 27, line 19, we add: 'It is for this reason that the Church is pleased that some lay people, married or single, imitate the example of the first Christians and join together, prudently and yet boldly, in such a way that all their goods are held in common, each receiving the portion of goods of which he has need and all living in the spirit of love and poverty. These forms of communitarian life should be warmly encouraged and renewed according to the spirit of the gospel especially among the peoples where they are still in force.'"

Conclusion

I have sometimes been told that the vocation to the community life is a special calling. No, it is simply the Christian and human vocation. People say to me, "The members of the existing communities must be exceptional people." Not at all. Knowing the members of the communities as well as I do, I can say that they are certainly ordinary mortals.

It's the present style of life which is extraordinary and abnormal; it is neither human nor beneficial for man. We have created a mass of tensions, the most important and the most crushing of which concerns money and its excessive importance. We think we can depend on an alleged equilibrium of opposing forces: capital-work; agriculture-industry, rich countries-poor countries; the arms race, etc. Isn't this utopian and insane? Doesn't it lead inevitably to catastrophe?

Members of communities are people like everyone else but they have understood the problem and the need to re-create the cells of humanity on a basis other than "the struggle of everyone against everyone else." Certainly the forms can and must vary according to the circumstances of place, time and actual needs: That's why the examples given above in no way exhaust the possibilities of communitarian reality. One reality, however, remains constant — the sharing at all levels, spiritual and material, from each according to his capacities (spiritual and material) to each according to his needs (spiritual and material).

A special vocation? I don't think so. Simply the acceptance of the truth. Man, every man, is called to a community. And the possibility of realizing a community in order to show men the way is the gift of God to every Christian: The only question for him is whether he accepts or rejects it. This is the truth of the matter. Community renewal in this last third of the 20th century can no longer be the task of a few experimental groups. It is a movement on which mankind's future depends, a movement which ought to embrace the whole world and primarily the Churches (because of the message of which they are the trustees).

CHAPTER 3

THE HIERARCHICAL OFFICES

1. The Diversity of Offices

We should say a few words now about the hierarchical offices which exist in the Christian community. My aim is not to write a theology of these offices but to place them in the total context of community life, according to some characteristic aspects which are perhaps too often forgotten. We will, moreover, attempt to do no more than offer suggestions for reflection.

The Christian community is a community of priests. It is important for us to repeat this fact here because, despite all that has been written on this subject, many still are afraid to believe it. In addition, a confusion about terms has greatly helped to introduce an error into the Christian mentality. The English word "priest" comes neither from the Greek word *hiereus* (which we translate "priest") nor from the Latin word *sacerdos* (which we likewise translate "priest"). It comes from the Koine Greek word *presbyteros* which means "elder," "president of the assembly." During the first two centuries, the words *hiereus* and *sacerdos* were attributed exclusively to Christ and Christians, never to the bishop or *presbyteros* (priest). These last were considered solely as the holders of an office within an assembly of priests.

I do not wish to deny or devaluate the functional priesthood of the bishops and clergy, but to see them in proper relationship to the universal priesthood of Christian joined to Christ, the priest. Nor do I want to say that in the Church the president of the assembly is simply the delegate of all, the one chosen by all. If he can celebrate the Eucharist in the midst of the community it is because, in addition to the choice of the sacerdotal community, he has received the imposition of hands from above which has qualified him to act in Christ's name in the act of sacrifice to the Father.

So, like any other living body, the Christian community, the priestly people, cannot subsist without a diversification of its functions. In particular, it needs a head, a leader — obviously it is Christ, but Christ present in the community and in each of its members. This leader communicates something of his service to the bishop, to the priests who are his extensions, and likewise to the deacons.

We would do well to recall a brief passage of the dogmatic *Constitution on the Church:*

And if by the will of Christ some are made teachers, dispensers of mysteries, and shepherds on behalf of others, yet all share a true equality with regard to the dignity and to the activity common to all the faithful for the building up of the Body of Christ . . . This very diversity of graces, ministries, and works gathers the children of God into one, because all these things are the work of one and the same Spirit (Art. 32).

Equality for all on the basis of the Christian state; diversity of functions within the community; unity of the body through the diversity of functions.

The Council even recalls the well-known words of St. Augustine:

> What I am for you terrifies me; what I am with you consoles me. For you I am a bishop; but with you I am a Christian. The former is a title of duty; the latter, one of grace. The former is a danger; the latter, salvation (Art. 32).

At the head of a community, or rather at the head of a community of communities, there is the bishop who has received the mission to teach these communities, who sanctifies them through the sacraments and who governs them. He answers to Christ for them. While being the head of a particular Church, the bishop is part of the college of bishops which is the head of the whole Church. Within this college of bishops, then, each bishop participates in the teaching, sanctification and government of the whole Church which is a great community of communities. The episcopal college has a leader, the bishop of Rome, who has primacy over all and possesses full, supreme and universal power in the Church (Art. 22).

Priests participate in the sacerdotal ministry in a secondary role. Around their bishop, and together with him, they form a *presbyterium* or college of presbyters. The presbyterium is really the bishops' co-workers, in those local communities which the bishop himself is not able to serve directly. They cooperate with the bishop. They do not, however, replace him. Here is a brief text from the *Constitution on the Church* on the mission of priests in local communities:

> Let them, as fathers in Christ, take care of the faithful whom they have spiritually begotten by bap-

tism and by their teaching. Having become from the heart a pattern to the flock, let them so lead and serve their local community that it may worthily be called by that name by which the one and entire People of God is distinguished, namely, the Church of God (Art. 28).

Let us then commend the dismemberment of huge dioceses and the increased number of bishops. Since the Council the bishop can no longer be that distant Excellency, a kind of administrator who gives "jurisdiction" to his priests without ever hearing confessions and who preaches the good news only through pastoral letters. It is primarily the bishop's responsibility to celebrate the Eucharist and the sacraments in the midst of his people and to proclaim and explain the word of God to them. He has a paternal role, but this presupposes that he has first of all become the brother of his lay brothers and sisters. Since priests do not replace the bishop but are only his co-workers, he himself must enter into the arena where the daily life of his brothers, of all men, is played out.

We have not said anything about the deacons yet. They share in the lower degree of the hierarchy. They receive the imposition of hands (which is a sacrament) not for the service of the people of God in the sacerdotal ministry but for the service of the people of God in certain liturgical functions, in the proclamation of the word of God, the instruction of Christians and catechumens. Their role is to preside over certain prayer meetings, the sharing of goods for charity, and the administration and even the material direction of the community.

2. Understanding These Offices in Relation to the Eucharist

The bishop and priests are really head of the community in Christ's name. We cannot understand their mission unless we start with the Eucharist over which they preside. The Eucharist is the mystery of the death and resurrection of Jesus and the announcement of his return; it is the sacrifice of Christ and his body to God the Father; it is the mystery of our common salvation. In it the community is welded together and in it the community finds its expression. Through it the community is achieved and strengthened until the fullness of the kingdom of heaven. The presidency of the bishop or priest is indispensable in this solemn act of community life. It is their responsibility to make the word of God heard, to explain it in the Church's name, to show it actualized in the sacrament but also in both the concrete life of the community and the life of each individual. It is their responsibility to celebrate the Eucharist *in persona Christi* (in the name of Christ the head) putting into operation the priesthood of the Church as community. It is their responsibility to preside at the communion in the body and blood of Christ. The Eucharist contains in itself the essential of the threefold function of bishops (and also of priests) to teach, sanctify and govern.

From this central point which is the Eucharist, bishops and priests continue their service to the community. They are the ministers of most of the sacraments, although some of these can be administered by deacons (baptism, distribution of communion) or by the laity (baptism in cases of necessity, marriage). It is principally their responsibility to present the word of God in different situations, to instruct Christians and

92

catechumens, to preside at prayer meetings and meals, but these ministries may be assumed by deacons, and laymen may also perform them according to needs and possibilities. It is primarily their responsibility to stimulate the community as a whole and each one in particular in spiritual matters, but they cannot do this unless they listen attentively to the way the Holy Spirit speaks to each of the members. If they are attentive to the words of the Holy Spirit in the least of their brethren they will be able to preside over the exchanges of charity, the mutual communication of the Spirit, the evangelical insights which are at the core of the community life, with truthfulness, respect and love.

Consequently, to the degree that we enter into the life which the Eucharist stimulates, each of us is bound to assume his particular responsibilities according to the mission and graces he has received. And when we touch on the numerous aspects of the life of the community which are strictly material, the bishop and the priest are disengaged from all responsibility, strictly speaking, except for the spiritual implications of material problems, for example, the safeguarding of poverty, charity in the sharing of goods, etc. Who, then, is responsible for the direction and material organization of the community and the allotment and sharing of material goods? The deacons, if there are any, or laymen. They do not replace the bishop or the priests — they fulfill their own role.

Certainly the mission of the laity also extends to the liturgy and even to the eucharistic mystery — and, need we mention, the apostolate! But it is not my intention to speak of these things here because in this chapter I am considering only the strictly hierarchical offices.

3. Hierarchical Offices and Authority

We must, first of all, make an important observation. The bishop, the priests (and even deacons) are not just ordinary assembly chairmen. They are not presidents only because everyone consents to this even if (as we would like) they should happen to be elected as in times past. Because the truth is that if they can preside over the life of the community it is because they have received the episcopal or presbyterial mission from on high through the sacrament of orders. When the Christian community is authentic it brings forth, as a law of life, members who are capable of receiving the sacred responsibilities of the episcopate, priesthood and diaconate which are, however, conferred on these only by an act of God in the sacrament of orders. As members of the communities the bishop, priest and deacon are Christ's gift to the community. The community receives all that it has from above, and especially its ministers.

As we can see, the community as such does not need a chaplain. The bishop and the priests, whose work allows his ministry to be extended, are first of all Christians and therefore brothers, but they have the office of leader. Every human community has always needed a head (either one person or a group) which it doubtlessly chose itself but which it recognized as a real authority and without which it could not subsist. This applies even more in the Christian community. Because of the fear of clericalism, whose roots we will consider later, some prefer to see the priest as a sort of chaplain. This is a bad thing for both the community and the priest. In fact, I know of many cases where a community or a group trying to become a community chose a lay president even for the spiritual domain without really thinking

94

about what it was doing because it considered the priest simply as a chaplain. I said to one of these presidents: "Have yourself ordained by your bishop." If the Church wants to become itself again, it must rediscover the whole truth about things, offices and persons.

Except in irregular and serious circumstances, members of a community owe obedience to those brethren who have received particular offices but only in the area of these offices. "Obey your leaders and do as they tell you, because they must give an account of the way they look after your souls" (Heb 13:17). The bishop and the priest have the right to obedience inasmuch as they have received the mission to be the guardians of tradition. In obeying them the community obeys an inner necessity of the faith itself. When we say that the bishop or the priest who extends his ministry is the guardian of tradition, this tradition shouldn't be understood as something finished and dead. On the contrary, tradition is the life which develops by contact with new realities but in faithful continuation of what it has always been.

One of the principal tasks of a bishop or a priest in the community is to find out how the Spirit is speaking to each community member, discerning the authenticity of what is said by confronting it with living tradition, and then gathering all this together, and "recapitulating" it for the good of the whole body. The bishop and the priest receive a special grace from the Spirit, a special presence of the Spirit to be able to "recapitulate" everything. But this special presence of the Spirit wouldn't do them or others any good if they disregarded the Spirit's presence in each member of the community.

How badly deformed is our sense of authority and obedience to the Church! We have only one leader — Christ — and we are all children of God. If we have authority in the assembly of the children of the Father, let our first care consist in being attentive to the Spirit that speaks to them. He speaks to them by the events which make up their lives, by the talents that he gives them, by the needs that he makes them experience. Let us not impose our plans from top to bottom — the Spirit is never in a plan but always in the life of a community of brothers. If we discern the way that the Spirit speaks to each one for the building up of the whole body, we will discover at the same time the Spirit's plan which is the only authentic plan and the only one that can succeed. If we can rediscover these essential values, we will rediscover the real meaning of authority and the real meaning of obedience in the reality of the Christian community — that these two attitudes indicate a submissiveness for the welfare of the whole body. In addition, we will see our leaders lose what has been called a "responsibility complex" and see an increased concern on their part for the whole community.

Certainly, because we are sinners, there are inevitably going to be difficulties. But among those who really live their community membership, authority and obedience will not stifle the Spirit. Because one complements the other, both require a humility and self-detachment which allows the Spirit to freely manifest himself in everyone for the good of the whole community and for the good of each individual. On the contrary, outside of an authentic community, which presupposes reciprocal knowledge, sharing and a certain living together, authority almost inevitably becomes a constraint and obedience a servitude.

4. Clergy or Laity? No: Community!

Changing Our Outlook and Our Structures

All that has just been said about the role of the bishop and priests implies a profound change in our outlook and especially a recommunitarization of the Church starting from the grass roots. We are so accustomed to thinking of the Church as an organization that we cannot imagine the structure other than it is now: a pyramid of different classes — laity, religious, clergy. Instead of a fraternal community with a mixture of different offices and charisms the Church has become a stratified organization like all organizations — with different layers and even different castes. This situation falsifies the role of the members of the hierarchy and creates a widespread uneasiness among Christians and particularly among priests. If we quickly diagnose this predicament, we might be in a better position to find a solution to the problem.

Since the French Revolution the clergy have lost, and are still losing, one after the other, all their temporal functions and prerogatives. They are of no "use" in the secular city. Therefore, they ask themselves two questions: What is our exact mission in the Church since only this mission can justify our existence? What is our place in the world today?

First of all, the priest today no longer concretely understands his place in the Church. Certainly the Council told him several times that he was sent by God to bring the word and the sacraments to men. But aren't there many laymen who can bring the word more pertinently and in a more down-to-earth way? And sometimes with more learning as well? The Eucharist and

97

most of the other sacraments are said to be reserved for the priest. But indeed this prerogative doesn't seem to him altogether a positive point. In fact, these sacraments are all the more cut off from ordinary life and its symbols because the priest who presides over the liturgical ceremonies is absent from this life. He forms a liturgical group around himself. What will his role be?

Will the priest fall back on the apostolate? On the missions? Not really — laymen seem better adapted and more efficient than he. In Catholic action he will be only the chaplain. In charitable works he will be the spiritual animator. What does that mean?

At least, we think, the priest governs the people of God in the bishop's name. But now he has to be assisted by a parish council which will very soon become all-powerful even though it has only a consultative vote. Can the priest morally make a decision which opposes that of the council? And if he does, what good is a council? To inform him? Laymen are adults and they have no desire to be simply informants.

The priest will then apply himself preferably to spiritual direction. That is his private domain. Not at all. The practice of the Oriental Church, for example, shows us that this mission is not peculiar to priests. Besides, the priest should take into account that Christian psychologists and psychoanalysts are performing miracles where he often worked without any apparent result.

Next, the priest no longer understands his place in today's world. He feels himself a stranger in it. While the leader of a community involved in the world, he has become a kind of monk. His celibacy, his nonparticipation in men's efforts to construct the city, all serve to isolate him from the world that it is his task principally — let us repeat *his* — to Christianize. In addition, his
98

studies still too often keep him apart from the human situation today and prevent him from being open to the great intellectual currents of our time.

Will the priest fasten himself to his bishop to join him and the presbyterium and find there a renewal of strength and the value of his existence? He doesn't think it likely. He knows that the bishop and his fellow priests have the same problems as he and he fears, above all, the proud isolation of a clerical corps which is even more cut off from the Christian laity and the world. Sometimes the incomprehension of some members of the hierarchy, or even the overwork of his own bishop, crushed by the worries of an immense diocese, keeps him from seeking the contacts and unity that he needs from this side.

That's not all. Today's priests know that throughout the world they are fewer in numbers and older in years. Priests know these facts and no one can blame them for feeling somewhat anxious. What kind of a boat are they in, anyway? Have they been trapped into assuming a burden which is more and more inhuman until their race is extinct? A bishop who is troubled about this situation recently told his priests: "Work confident that when you die I won't have anyone to replace you." What enthusiasm can you have for a task when you know that no one is going to carry on the work? Granted, the ordination of deacons is happening. But we know very well that deacons are not intended to make up for the lack of priests. The diaconate is a different office from the priesthood. A pastor of 12 parishes recently told me that his communities each needed a priest but not necessarily a deacon. That could be discussed.

This uneasiness on the part of the clergy has been too briefly described. Each point most certainly deserves a long explanation. Before we outline the prospect for the future, let's recall that this great suffering is and must be the whole body's. Christians who have received sacerdotal ordination have accepted it for the good of the body, for the service of the whole Church and each of their brethren. It would be altogether abnormal if the laity — as the people of God are called — should be indifferent to this urgent problem and not feel its impact strongly.

The most urgent matter, it would seem, is to give priests a hope that will reanimate them. Without that the situation is in danger of getting worse. Priests must be made to realize that the future, even here below, is brighter than they think. The whole Church must be able to glimpse this earthly future so as to be ready to accept the changes which the future will demand.

A bishop said some time ago, "My priests want to become laymen and my laymen want to become priests." It was just a literary device for the purpose of pointing out that Christians, priests and laymen, are looking for the truth in the midst of the present confusion.

Basically, the opposing terms clergy-laity refer to an organizational and Constantinian conception of the Church.

It is a fact that when men turn aside from community life they spontaneously organize themselves into classes, even into all kinds of castes. This is a historical fact. We don't have to examine the causes of this in depth here but we can easily understand that when each one lives in his own corner without knowing or being known, without that oneness of soul which makes him share, men will only unite by virtue of those laws and constraints which presuppose or create classes and castes. The community itself has never known classes, social or otherwise, and yet it has always recognized the need of a leader or a group of leaders who, while having extensive powers, are first of all brothers among their brothers. The tensions between episcopate and presbyterate, episcopate and laity, presbyterate and laity, are typical of a Church somewhat "decommunalized." Our dioceses, our parishes, our associations are scarcely communities. In the present system it is hard for laymen, for example, to know the bishop, the priest, as one among them who has received a special character and grace to preside over the life of their community while remaining principally one of them, burdened by the same problems, the same difficulties, and leaning on them just as they lean on him. Instead of communities where each one has his own role to play for the good of others there are now, whether we like it or not, more or less castes. Instead of being a community of communities the Church is more or less stratified — there is the stratum of the laity, the stratum of the priesthood and the stratum of the episcopate. Tensions between these castes or strata are inevitable and they can be resolved only by a return to a more authentic community life.

Since the prelate mentioned above was allowed his little witticism, I'd like to be allowed mine. Here it is — "In place of the clergy, give us many priests."

For, after all, there is neither clergy nor laity. This stratification didn't exist in the first centuries of the Church. There are only Christian communities. Or rather there *should* be only Christian communities — that's the whole problem. In these communities there are men who, brothers among their brothers, have been called by God and by the community (which comes to the same thing) to fulfill the functions of the priesthood. These men are members of the people of God, living in the same conditions as all their brethren, sharing the same culture, the same work, the same cares. But they have been chosen to be presbyters, i.e., elders. The bishop, having recognized their aptitudes for this function, has imposed his hands on them and as a result they have received supernally the indelible grace to preside over the people. Their ministry is sacred. But this choice and this grace in no way separate them from the Christian people. Nor in this way do they become members of a clerical class, but rather are made the trustees of an office within the assembly.

Can the communities consequently not put forward their own requirements which change according to time, place and circumstances in the choice of their priests? Can Christian communities of workers not demand that their priests be workers (not priest-workers but worker-priests) as Bishop Ancel has suggested? Can a community conscious of certain difficulties not choose a priest more in touch with the advances of modern psychology, if it would be useful to do so? One time a group of Christians said that their wish was to have priests who were at least 40 years old! This is somewhat understandable; it isn't easy to be an elder at 24 years of age. Let's recognize quite frankly that in many cases the ordination of good laymen over 40 would be better for the community than the launching into space of a young man who has no experience of life at all. Because grace doesn't suppress nature but presupposes it, the sacrament of orders requires an adequate human base. Who would dare deny this? Certainly a theological formation is needed, but must everyone acquire this in a seminary?

Let us say in passing that we must rediscover the value of the divine call to accept the burden of the priesthood, which is contained in the call which the community and its bishop address to one of its members.

Besides, the seminaries are emptying. This isn't tragic. On the contrary, this is a sign from the Spirit we must humbly recognize. Why don't young men want to enter the seminary? Because they are afraid of the obligation of celibacy? Some, yes. But in general doesn't their refusal come from their unwillingness to become part of a class, a caste of Christian society? They wouldn't be unwilling to be chosen as priests of their community and to be consecrated to this ministry, but they are unwilling to join the ranks of the clergy. Fortunately there are still young men who decide and accept to make the step. These men are working to effectively change the structures from within.

The future of the clergy as such is grim, while that of the Christian communities is full of promise and, to the degree that these communities become genuine, they will see members formed from within who are capable with God's grace of taking on the functions of the priesthood. The criteria the communities will use in choosing priests will no doubt be different from the canonical standards of today but, no less demanding, they will better express the actual needs of the communities.

What About Episcopal Collegiality?

We might wonder how this view of the Church fits in with the collegiality of the bishops. Isn't it the college of bishops with the pope, that is, if I may use the expression, the episcopal "class" which is the Church's supreme authority?

No! The college of bishops is not a class of higher clergy! It's precisely in the reality of the Church as "community of communities" that collegiality is really comprehensible and beneficial. The Council put it this way:

> The individual bishop, however, is the visible principle and foundation of unity in his particular Church, fashioned after the model of the universal Church. In and from such individual Churches there comes into being the one and only Catholic Church. For this reason each individual bishop represents his own Church, but all of them together in union with the Pope represent the entire Church joined in the bond of peace, love, and unity (*Lumen Gentium*, art. 23).

The bishops with the pope are the head of the whole Church, that is, of the great community of communities, because they are the leaders of local communities. The direction of the total community can only be collegial (with the pope as leader of the college) because, for the sake of total community, each local community has a character and a unique value (the Church is there in all its fullness) and is an indispensable member of the whole body without which the body would not be able to be what it is. Collegiality takes on the full weight of its meaning to the degree that the Churches become authentic communities.

In addition, is it really necessary to add that "destratification" of the Church, and consequently a decentralization at all levels for the benefit of "basic communities," as well as a correct and full sense of collegiality, would very much favor ecumenical progress and the unity of all Christians?

Note on the Common Life of Priests

It is normal and desirable for the bishop to live in the same dwelling as not only his councillors but also with the priests of the "basic community" which in particular is his responsibility. It is normal that the celibate priests of the same community live together in the same house. The canonical style of priestly life, which has a long history and is full of lessons, deserves very careful study.[13] The conciliar texts more than once encourage the common life of priests:

> . . . community life for priests is strongly recommended, especially for those attached to the same parish. While this way of living encourages apostolic action, it also affords an example of charity and unity to the faithful (Decree on *The Pastoral Office of Bishops,* art. 30, no. 1).

> . . . cultivate kindliness and share their goods in common. They will be particularly solicitous for priests who are sick, afflicted. . . . Furthermore, in order that priests may find mutual assistance in the development of their spiritual and intellectual lives, that they may be able to cooperate more effectively in their ministry and be saved from the dangers which may arise from loneliness, let there be fostered among them some kind or other of community life. Such a life can take on several forms according to various personal or pastoral needs: for instance, a shared roof where this is feasible, or a common table, or at least frequent and regular gatherings (Decree on *The Priestly Life and Ministry,* art. 8).

> After the example of that communion of goods which was praised in the history of the primitive Church, some common use of things can pave the way to pastoral charity in an excellent manner. Through this form of living, priests can laudably reduce to practice the spirit of poverty recommended by Christ (*Ibid.,* art. 17).

We can see that despite the nuances involved, the Council openly pushes priests towards community life. For this we can be grateful. However, it seems to me important to underline that a priestly community is not strictly speaking a community but the head of a community, the great majority of whose members are laymen. A priest's community is his lay community, not the next pastor who is president of another community. Therefore, when a community has only one priest it is normal that he lives in *it* and not with a group of priests each of whom is responsible for a different community. On the contrary, when a community has many priests it is completely normal for them to live together if they are unmarried. However, once again a priestly college does not exist to be a community — it is a member of a community — its head.

It is very important that we take care to preserve this reality because otherwise we are raising obstacles to true community renewal and we are falling back into the stratification of the Church. Therefore, from this point of view the college of priests must share spiritually and materially with the whole community. Their prayer (office) must be that of the whole community and, even if it happens that they say it without the other brethren participating, they remain nonetheless the delegates of the whole community in the service of God.

CHAPTER 4

RELIGIOUS IN THE CHURCH
AS COMMUNITY

1. The Problem

Many think that chapter 6 of the Constitution *Lumen Gentium* (On Religious) and the Decree on the *Renewal of the Religious Life* have not really defined the religious life, nor offered anything new. Both, however, open the way to a fruitful inquiry. Nonetheless, they do relate the religious life to the life of the whole Church and they do insist on the insertion of religious congregations into the one body of Christ. The religious life appears as a more intense ecclesial life, as the heart of this great body which is animated by the Spirit.

We know that historically the cenobitic life (which gave birth to the religious life) was the result of the desire to rediscover the *vita apostolica,* that is, the common life that Jesus lived with his disciples, the life of the Jerusalem community and also the life which the Church lived in different degrees of intensity throughout the first three centuries of its existence. The first and the essential ideal of religious is to follow Christ (*sequela*

Christi) in a communitarian life (*koinonia*). Basically the cenobites, and after them the religious, have preserved this ideal, which belongs to all Christians, by consecrating it and giving it a social, institutional, and in some degree, a strengthened character.

Consequently, these communities from the age of Constantine to the present have sometimes siphoned off for themselves, without realizing it, the community ideal which belongs to the whole Church. What characterizes the religious life is precisely that it is a community strengthened to safeguard and maintain *koinonia* in the Church.

These religious communities are trying to reform themselves and to provide new constitutions for themselves. But is it conceivable that they should do this today without taking into consideration the move of the "ordinary" Church towards community?

Somewhere between the Church's search for community and the renewal of the religious life there is a point of convergence which we must discover in practice.

2. Complementary Communities

There are at present two types of complementary Christian communities — the religious communities and the ordinary communities. What distinguishes one from the other? Are religious communities separated from the world, whereas ordinary communities are part of the world? This is certainly not what distinguishes them because some religious communities are more in the world and more active than some lay communities. This is a question of a special vocation. Or is it that, on the one hand, celibacy is the mark and sign of consecration to the Lord, while, on the other, marriage is the normal and ordinary way? But in that case the distinction is not specific, because virginity isn't the exclusive property of religious (there are many celibates in the ordinary communities, and married Christians also live an authentic spiritual virginity in imitation of Christ and his mother). Is the difference poverty? You have to know the poverty and the effective interdependence and material insecurity reigning in some nonreligious communities to realize that many convents have much to learn on this subject in imitating them . . . either that, or they are Pharisees who falsify the meaning of the words they use.

The distinction seems to me to lie in the special status that religious claim, which gives them the mission to reveal to the eyes of all — we might say officially — the community ideal which belongs to the whole Church on its way towards the community of the kingdom of heaven. Religious communities have norms approved and imposed by the Church which enable them to "preserve" for the good of all the community life which ought to animate all Christians and in this way reveal the ultimate community. On the other hand, among ordinary Christians, except for the great principles governing the unity of the Body of Christ, community life takes on freer forms, forms which are more spontaneous, more varied, and which can be adapted to suit the real needs of the world as it is here and now.

They are complementary communities of the same people of God! This is shown, among other ways, by the fact that all these communities are placed by the Lord under the care of the same bishop in the same way. And if some religious communities escape from the jurisdiction of the local bishop (except for what touches pastoral or apostolic matters) this "privilege" of exemption (which will no longer be needed on the day that each one respects and loves the proper vocation of the other) does not liberate these religious communities from the authority of the hierarchy but, rather, places them under the direct authority of the pope.

3. Working Towards Integrated Communities

The Future of the Religious Life

The complementarity of the two types of communities cannot be verified by keeping them in watertight compartments. On the contrary, it presupposes sharing. But precisely because the Church of today is seeking community life, we wonder if this sharing wouldn't be better realized by integrating the religious communities into the ordinary communities of the Christian people.

The religious life is, as it were, the heart of the Church:

Then arises their duty of working to implant and strengthen the kingdom of Christ in souls and to extend that kingdom to every land. This duty is to be discharged to the extent of their capacities and in keeping with the form of their proper vocation. The chosen means may be prayer or active undertakings. . . . The profession of the evangelical counsels, then, appears as a sign which can and ought to attract all the members of the Church to an effective and prompt fulfillment of the duties of their Christian vocation (*Lumen Gentium,* no. 44).

Isn't this Christian vocation essentially communitarian? Isn't it the following of Christ together in the *koinonia*? The Church itself is made up of communities; we would like to see the religious, in the concrete reality of day-to-day living, be the heart of these basic communities which form the Church of Christ.

For a Christian community to be formed and in order for it to live it needs a nucleus. Isn't this the primary role of the religious community? It isn't a community for itself, but the heart of the Christian community. Can a heart beat for the benefit of the whole body when it's locked away in a closed jar? They tell me that religious pray a great deal and do many apostolic works. Granted, but are they sufficiently the heart of the prayer of the Christian community? Are they sufficiently the soul of the Christian community's apostolic work? More than that, do they have enough opportunities to communicate to Christians the style of community life which is the basis of the vocation they have in common? When can Christians eat a meal with them, when can they share with them spiritually, when can they pray with them (without being cut off from them), when can they pool their goods with them? Shouldn't we be seeking these things? It's not enough that Sister So-and-so is a nurse in the area, or a social worker — what is needed is that the community of sisters agree to be only an organ — the heart — of a Christian community that it helps to live and to shape.

And so new perspectives for the religious life are developing.

The ordinary community finds it necessary to have some members in it who will remain celibates. Called by God and consecrated to him and to the community directly, they do not live on the two levels of family life and community life like the other members, but only on the community level to which they are exclusively dedicated.

According to their charismatic gifts, their own particular vocation and the needs of the community, they will be reserved voluntarily for the praise of God or for works which are directly apostolic. They will offer unceasing prayer to God in which the members who are married and engaged in the business of the world will join when they are able.

Their poverty, like that of the other members, will consist first of all in the fraternal sharing of material resources. But while the ordinary members will have the worry of managing their own goods and those of the community, the religious by God's will and the community's, will be freed from this worry.

They will depend for their needs on their brothers and sisters and will have no need to be concerned about their livelihood, although this will not dispense them from the obligation to work with other men for the building of the secular city. This total detachment will be a sign for all of the unrestricted wealth of the kingdom of heaven which is yet to come and yet already present.

Their obedience, which will be for each the imitation of Christ's obedience to his Father, will demonstrate a more perfect love of the community through a greater service of it.

To sum up — religious will be the nuclear group but not a community in itself — around which the whole community will live and develop. And it is the whole community as such which will be "not of" the world but in the world. In this way then the false antithesis between the "religious life" and the "world" is resolved, for all Christians through their baptism have left the world and entered into the community of salvation, and their separation from the world is for the salvation of the world and enables them to be present in it as leaven. There is no need, then, for the religious to separate themselves in daily life from the other members of the community. The only actual separation will be on the basis of the special functions the community attributes to the group of male or female religious. The community will set apart an area which will give them the opportunity to have peace and silence which are indispensable and a place to live which will foster their encounter with the Lord, particularly if they are religious dedicated to contemplation and the praise of God.

Nonetheless, religious remain brothers and sisters among their lay brothers and sisters. We must do away with everything that hinders contact as well as everything that keeps Christians and non-Christians from finding, in religious, men and women like themselves. Isn't it time in many cases to get rid of useless barriers such as high walls, grills, special costumes? We might ask ourselves, for example, if certain habits ". . . be suited to the circumstances of time . . . and the services required by those who wear them" (Decree on *The Religious Life,* no. 17).

I have been asked more than once what would be the function of religious institutions, orders or congregations. It seems to me logical that consecrated members, who belong to core groups which form the center of communities, should sometimes meet together and should be joined to some order or other. It seems to me that they should even have a special structure. Won't the superiors also have to specially watch over them in the name of the bishop? Is this incompatible with life in ordinary communities of Christian people? I don't think so. Obviously this presupposes a decentralization of these religious groups away from their superiors and their "mother houses" but won't that be good for everyone?

This renewal of community life in lay communities will give the religious an equilibrium and an openness that at the moment they find hard to discover because of frictions within their groups. Now if a religious has some trouble, she is transferred. . . . If she is too attached, she is transferred. (There is, however, an attachment which is necessary, fulfilling, from the Spirit and good for the heart.) Experience shows that the problems of religious life are best resolved by the opening of these communities and their insertion as a particular organ (the heart) in a large lay community. When this is done, we must accept that religious weave strong ties with their brothers and sisters in the community. For example, chastity consecrated to God is more peaceful and more fulfilling for religious who have the possibility of frequently sharing deeply with their married brothers and sisters, of entering into their worries and joys, and who reveal their own difficulties and achievements to them and really become their brothers and sisters.

We are convinced that in these circumstances religious vocations would again be numerous even though today a simple statistical calculation forces us to conclude that in the near future there will be a considerable numerical reduction of religious in the Church.

If only religious would understand this! If they would agree to put the communitarian treasure they possess — often without realizing it — at the service of the Church and the Church's basic communities there would really be a revolution! They could forcefully help the Church to become again a community of communities. They could inculcate in Christians that social order at once new and ancient which was preached by Christ, lived by him and his disciples and put into practice during the first three centuries of the Church. And men who seek for a point of reference, who wonder where to look, would have something to see when they saw our communities. We would give them an idea of how to build a secular city which is more fraternal and therefore more human.[14]

Evidently this requires a profound change of mentality and of the structures of "religious life." But, on the other hand, it is only by beginning now that these changes will gradually be achieved. I know many groups which have started the slow work of integration. Two of these religious, living in Montreal, were told recently by one family of their community: "You've finally become our sisters. . . ." We have called them "Sisters" for centuries but it was just a title we gave them; it didn't really mean what it said.

Everything moves quickly today and it's time to get to work. And for religious to get to work doesn't mean first of all to draw up new constitutions, but to concretely seek a way of becoming members of an ordinary community of the people of God on the basis of equality. Too often during my travels I have noticed that religious are working to elaborate new constitutions without really knowing what they are looking for. They don't have a precise goal or plan. Sometimes they don't even know what they still stand for in the Church today. This seems serious to me. But the plan is the construction of the Christian community and its stimulation by the active presence in it of consecrated brothers and sisters exclusively dedicated to it.

In Practice

On the practical level, each congregation should conduct experimental integration in those areas where

115

the laity desires a community. Such efforts of adult religious should be closely followed by their superiors and backed up by research organizations.

How should religious proceed? It is a question we're often asked. This depends on circumstances. A "life together" which permits an authentic spiritual and material sharing with the other members of the Christian community must get started. The concrete forms of this life together have to be decided by the lay members as well as by the religious members. They must proceed gradually. This presumes, above all, on the part of the religious, a determined will to become brothers and sisters of their brothers and sisters, to work with them, to share their cares, their joys, their sufferings and to receive from them as much as they give. When we live with this spirit and this truth, we quickly understand the steps that must be taken and we immediately seize hold of events which favor the growth of the community. In this way a pattern of meals taken together, prayer gatherings and liturgical celebrations is easily recognized. They listen to the word of God together so that together they may understand what the Lord expects of the community. Little by little, they practice the revisions of community life.

Certainly we have to be humble. It would be hard for most religious and ordinary Christians to achieve this sharing right now. This doesn't matter. The Church moves forward because of minorities, so does the world. Besides, experience proves that every community is formed of concentric circles. At the center there is a group of committed families and single people, including some religious. Around this group there is a circle of noncommitted members, a large circle of friends and helpers in this or that material, spiritual or apostolic

116

enterprise of the community . . . next the parish, and then the world. No one is excluded, but some go further than others in the commitment. No one feels left out since everything is done in love which the Holy Spirit inspires.

Parallel to this work of integrating some groups of religious, a wholesale decentralization of the structure of congregations must be accomplished. These congregations should allow their religious to become full members of ordinary communities of the Christian people, that is, to share spiritually and materially with their brothers and sisters in these communities. This will not harm these congregations, quite the contrary. They will no doubt acquire a renewed sense of purpose but, more important, what they offer their religious will be closer to the real because of the many experiences of community life they will have lived with laymen.

On the other hand, all the communities belonging to congregations which are searching must try to live in a more communitarian way because they know that *koinonia* is the very essence of their vocation. Among other things, the huge communities must be broken up into smaller groups with allowance made for each one to really know and be known — the "primary relations" are all the more necessary because the religious community ought to be, by its vocation, an intense kind of community.

I sometimes hear the objection that all this doesn't concern the religious who are contemplatives. In my opinion, this is wrong. Even groups of contemplatives (once they are small) ought to enter into a sharing with laymen. Sometimes they can become part of communities where the prayer life is sufficiently developed and where the lay members understand the consecration of their brethren to the service of God in the contemplation of his face. I know a group of Carmelites who are trying to live in community with lay people and a Trappist monastery which is also doing this. But a community is also possible in the case of contemplative nuns — lay people must be able to pray with these sisters, share with them spiritually (fortunately the grills are gone), and to share also materially. Lay people should know how their sisters, who are dedicated to prayer, live and what they need so that they can take care of these needs by sharing. Some Carmelite nuns would be only too happy to be able to help mothers of families by doing the washing for them.

The "recommunitarization" of the Church is a movement that nothing can stop. Religious should participate in this by utilizing all their possibilities and potentialities which still are very considerable. They could change the face of the Church and resolve the problem of the religious life in today's world.

CHAPTER 5

THE CHURCH AS COMMUNITY AND THE WORLD

1. The Church as Community and the Construction of the World

The Principles

The Church is a historical reality resulting from a special intervention of God in the world. God has saved the world through his son Jesus Christ who was born, died and rose again and who constituted a body through the sending of the Spirit. Through this body, Christ prolongs his salvific action among all men. The Church, the body of Christ, is truly a priestly people: In him, who is the unique mediator, it participates in the salvation of the world; in him, who is the unique light, it illumines the world and shows it the way to happiness and salvation. Looking at the Church, human society should see the road which leads to perfection.

Let us first of all take a look at some passages of the pastoral constitution *The Church in the Modern World*.

United on behalf of heavenly values and enriched by them, this family has been constituted and organized in the world as a society by Christ, and is equipped with those means which befit it as a visible and social unity. Thus the Church, at once a visible assembly and a spiritual community, goes forward together with humanity and experiences the same earthly lot which the world does. She serves as a leaven and as a kind of soul for human society as it is to be renewed in Christ and transformed into God's family (*Gaudium et Spes,* no. 40, par. 2).

. . . the Church not only communicates divine life to men, but in some way casts the reflected light of that life over the entire earth . . . by her healing and elevating impact on the dignity of the person, by the way in which she strengthens the seams of human society. . . . Thus, through her individual members and her whole community, the Church believes she can contribute greatly toward making the family of man and its history more human (*Ibid.,* no. 40, par. 3).

Christ, to be sure, gave his Church no proper mission in the political, economic, or social order. The purpose which he set before her is a religious one. But out of this religious mission itself comes a function, a light, and an energy which can serve to structure and consolidate the human community according to the divine law (*Ibid.,* 42, par. 2).

For the promotion of unity belongs to the innermost nature of the Church, since she is, by her relationship with Christ, both a sacramental sign and an instrument of intimate union with God, and of the unity of all mankind. Thus she shows the world that an authentic union, social and external, results from a union of minds and hearts, namely, from that faith and charity by which her own unity is unbreakably rooted in the Holy Spirit. For the force which the

Church can inject into the modern society of man consists in that faith and charity put into vital practice . . . (*Ibid.,* 42, par. 3).

Hence the mission of the Church is not only to bring to men the message and grace of Christ, but also to penetrate and perfect the temporal sphere with the spirit of the gospel (*The Apostolate of the Laity,* no. 5).

In the course of history, temporal things have been foully abused by serious vices. Affected by original sin, men have frequently fallen into multiple errors concerning the true God, the nature of man, and the principles of the moral law. The result has been the corruption of morals and human institutions and not rarely contempt for the human person himself. . . . It is the task of the whole Church to labor vigorously so that men may become capable of constructing the temporal order rightly and directing it to God through Christ. . . . The temporal order must be renewed in such a way that, without the slightest detriment to its own proper laws, it can be brought into conformity with the higher principles of the Christian life . . . (*Ibid.,* no. 7).

Having read these conciliar texts, I would like to quote some sentences of G. Minette de Tillesse which may serve as encouragement and warning.

"The attitude of the Christian towards the world is not negative but prophetic. Like Isaiah of old who was a sign for his generation (Is 9, 18; Ez 4, 1-17) the Christian is also a living 'witness' of the Risen Christ. His life already anticipates the resurrection and this is why his whole being, his whole life is a sign and a prophetic testimony for the whole world.

"The Christian is not then a gloomy character who

121

resents progress but, on the contrary, an eschatological being who pushes towards the future. The Christian, even more than the Marxist, is a dynamic person who with all his spiritual enthusiasm draws the cosmos towards the future."[15]

Application

Actually, the communities of the Church find themselves facing human groups which differ widely one from the other.

On the one hand, there are associations which are authentic communities — their members are interiorly united by an underlying principle; the whole sees that each family and each individual has the goods that they need within the framework of a common ownership. When the Church finds itself faced with such communities, it has the duty to work to maintain them and to strengthen the profoundly human qualities which they have. Moreover, it should help these communities to go beyond their limitations and negative aspects through the Holy Spirit which it is able to breathe into them. Whether these communities are inspired by a natural solidarity, by an atheist ideology, or by tribal feeling, the Church should attentively and humbly show consideration for them, knowing that it has much to receive from their example and their experience.

But, more frequently, the Church confronts organizations which are not communities but which are indeed anticommunity. In capitalist regimes economics is built, in practice, on money as the highest value: Society lives by a continual tension between capital and work. Man is looked upon only as a producer and a consumer and not as a person. Technology, driven by the profit motive, often reduces man to the level of an instrument at the service of a faceless society. And when the State wants to curb laissez-faire capitalism, it does so by a dehumanizing centralized power. The problem is almost the same in socialist regimes in that, despite a certain equality, socialist man finds it dangerous to become an individual; state socialism, bureaucracy and technocracy threaten him. In both systems, the great progress achieved in the understanding of man is the mastery of the forces of nature, in techniques of all sorts which, in fact, tend to militate against man's liberation and his return to himself. Often they may even menace him physically, mentally and morally. The multitude of specializations at all levels tends to destroy "primary relations" among men (those which unite persons and which presuppose mutual knowledge) for the sake of secondary relations between individuals (those which group together only activities).

Most assuredly, in the midst of all this, voices are raised more and more strongly extolling a system of life centered on human values. Let us recall that Marxism is seeking the Communist synthesis — the reabsorption of the tensions between capital and labor, agriculture and industry, etc., which can be achieved, according to the leading Marxist philosophers, only by the restoration of the base communities where primacy will be given to human relationships. Teilhard de Chardin, for his part, proclaims a more and more complex "socialization" which is more and more conscious, but if we pay attention to what he puts under the term "socialization" we will see that he means, in fact, "communitarization." Indeed, what is about to be achieved, according to him, is not a union of human beings which touches only the periphery of themselves, but a joining of "center to center." We should analyze the "communitarian per-

123

sonalism" of E. Mounier. We should study the principles of the "European Federalist Movement."[16] We should point out the many efforts to discover the community which are evident right now in a country as socially fragmented as the United States. There are innumerable movements trying to reconstruct, along the lines of basic communities, the economic, political and religious life of this immense Babel. Granted that in this whole area we have only rough descriptions, yet it is still provable that in our socially fragmented world, whether capitalist or socialist, men are in search of something beyond, which is a truly human synthesis continually open and evolving. What men are looking for is the community.

However, we are still far from achieving community. And so we must ask, "What should the Church be doing in this world of ours?"

It should first of all be present to the world sympathetically, in order to know it and to share its life. Through its magisterium it should teach man's sovereign dignity and cry out against the palliatives applied to the law of profits, of interest and all the other tensions inherent in the system. It should promote man's salvation right in this society which seems to be falling apart and work for its evolution according to human and Christian principles. The Church has played this role and still does — think of the social encyclicals, the conciliar documents on *The Church in the Modern World* and on *The Apostolate of the Laity,* and the encyclical *Populorum Progressio.* Think especially of the many organized temporal activities of militant Christians. A Christian who really has a community sense can never lose interest in the struggle that is going on in the world under the pretext of having attained a certain "synthesis." This would be an inexcusable retreat. Let us hope that one who lives the community experience in his heart sees better than others a goal to reach for. This is all the more reason for him to get involved in the struggle with the full weight of his vision and his peace. With perseverance he should direct tensions towards a search for a synthesis and know how to sometimes choose the lesser evil in order to oppose the greater wrong.

But this isn't enough. In addition, the Church should show men, by all that the Church is, that the ultimate goal is none other than the earthly likeness and representation of the kingdom of heaven. To do this it should involve Christians in the establishment of wide open communities animated by the Holy Spirit. These should be full communities, that is, their mode of life should correspond to the total unity that the Spirit, animating the body of Christ, achieves in them. The Church should encourage her children to seek out the forms of community life which are adapted to our age and to the different regions of the globe. If the Church, which is a community, hears the voice of the Spirit and becomes once again conscious of what it is by establishing communities which are authentic and wide open, it will once more become what it ought to be for a world torn between two systems — the light.

Certainly we must not deny original sin, and the communities presuppose an unceasing victory over our egotism. However, if humanity wants to continue to exist it must move towards the community even it it can be foreseen that in many respects large sections of mankind will never really get that far. For mankind to be able to continue existing there is need of a *communitarian backbone*. Without these communities, which continually teach and show the way to follow, which help men to move towards the goal, there will be disaster.

In order to live, men need a reference point. To be able to construct the city they need to look towards a goal. But often this is the only profit derived from being a reference point. The kibbutzim of Israel contain only 4.5 percent of the population. Many Israeli do not want the life of the kibbutzim for themselves but everyone realizes that without the kibbutzim there wouldn't be an Israel. This is only a small example of the strength of communities even when they are imperfect on some points.

The Church's vocation is to be the world's spinal column because it is a human and divine community and announces the kingdom of heaven by fulfilling it already here below. In looking at the Church the world should see something it desires and feels the need of — something which helps in the establishment of the secular city itself. The Church is the body of Christ, the perfect community formed of communities, all animated by the Holy Spirit. The Church is this, but "this" ought to appear to the world's eyes in forms that the eyes of the world can see. If our unity brought about by the Spirit of Christ doesn't show itself in a visible mutual support, in an authentic sharing of material as well as spiritual goods, it is because our unity isn't genuine, our community isn't genuine, and then men who look for a path to follow can see nothing when they look at us; they are unable to receive any light from us. In these times of renewal we must ask ourselves if the world which looks at our parish communities and the rest can see something in them and find the light that they need there!

The confused world wonders where to look. Let us show it our communities. Certainly men will most often only imperfectly and remotely approach the ideal that we present to them (we ourselves also do so imperfectly) but they will be able to get started and the awareness of what they lack will be the beginning of their salvation.

The future of the world depends on Christians, on their fidelity to the gospel. They are truly the "soul of the world." When will they understand their responsibility? Only Christ can achieve real community because in him God has willed to *recapitulate* everything. Only faith in Christ as head of mankind can make men *live* in one body and *keep* them in one body. In fact, most men are not of the Christian faith, but even though they don't know it, Christians are a priestly people for their benefit. The Church can at least show them its teaching about the community, its community life, and they can proceed to find in this the light that they need. Indeed, in the world today, only Christianity possesses a truly communitarian and universal doctrine and spirituality which can gather men together without taking anything away from their personalities or the integrity of the family but on the contrary enhance these latter. Christianity has its "chance" now at the end of the 20th century. The Christian community is a full community and the light of the world, because the Spirit breathes his fullness into it. But still Christians must let the Spirit work.

One day Christ will return. Then all the divergent and contradictory forces which separate men from one another will be overcome and the community will triumph for eternity. The Lord's judgment will be shown in the definite establishment of the community and the definite abolition of the alienation in which mankind lives. But today the Church's mission is to witness to this communitarian fulfillment by its life. It should be an anticipation of the community of the kingdom of heaven, of that ideal community which, whether we like

127

it or not, whether we know it or not, men must try to imitate if they want to save themselves.

Note on the Community and World Peace

Violence? Nonviolence? The overwhelming problems which mankind faces force us to make a choice. But history has already made this choice for us. It is only too clear that violence provokes violence and sets off a chain reaction always involving the destruction of a greater number of men until today we have reached the point where the very existence of humanity can be endangered.

A community which is the world in miniature necessarily opts for active nonviolence, that is, for fraternal dialogue. If it didn't do this, it would destroy itself instantly.

A community lives when its members accept the other members as they are and not as they would like them to be; when they overcome their differences, not by harming one another but by deeply sharing and by synthesizing all the good that is in each of them; when they love enough to bear one another's sins, to heal one another, to strengthen one another.

This active nonviolence as lived in communities is the supreme violence because it alone conquers the kingdom of heaven. The world in which we live has been too often built on opposing tensions which have led to catastrophes, wars and famines. The community reorients men one towards the other, destroys tensions and builds humanity on the convergent forces of love. But this can only be achieved by a supreme violence, revolutionary ways of thinking and acting, self-criticism, persuasion, exchange and sharing.

Laissez-faire liberalism was established and is established by the kind of violence which crushes the weak for the profit of the strong and which continues to impoverish two thirds of the world for the benefit of the rich countries. Socialism was established and is established by the kind of violence which crushed the owners for the profit of an anonymous and impersonal State which pretends to be the savior of all and the supplier of the needs of all. The community is the desired synthesis, and because it is a synthesis it can be established only by active nonviolence which brings all men together and reunites all the values contained in the thesis and antithesis.

Marxist philosophers have clearly explained how capitalism gives way to socialism, namely, by violent revolution. The new doctrine, according to which socialism can come about without a violent revolution, has never been tested in reality and would seem to be inapplicable. Besides, it is the product of the compliance of the rich countries, that is, of those countries where everyone profits from the poverty of the Third World. But nowhere in the works of Marxist theoreticians is it explained how to pass from socialism to communism. We can understand their embarrassment. Synthesis signifies general good will, transcending egotism, and the building of a fraternal city where all the riches of the total man and of all mankind will be assembled in a mutual, personal and consequently free gift.

The temptation of violence is great among these people who are under dictatorship built on the power of money. I don't say that, considering the extreme character of the situation, violent revolution is not justified in their case but that revolution will not solve everything because the synthesis we earnestly desire will never be the direct result of violence and destruction.

Because communities achieve a synthesis out of their active nonviolence they are eminently adapted to play a role in the building of the world of tomorrow. They must become conscious of this. They must expressly train themselves to live their active nonviolence and their fraternal dialogue, not only among themselves, but also in their relations with those outside.

Let us take two closely related examples — the violence of money and the violence of weapons.

Our economic regime is entirely based on the alleged supposition that capital is the highest value. Many recent studies have shown with unequalled force that usury (the automatic interest that money is thought to produce) is a fundamental error. We have long been deceived about its legitimacy. Now it appears as the major coercion which the rich have over the poor and the men of today have over those of tomorrow. In economics, interest on money is the ultimate weapon. We can certainly conclude that the countries of the Third World will not take their place among the developed nations of the earth as long as they are kept at their mercy by an economic regime based on usury as a constraint and on money as the highest good.

The dictatorship of money is also evident in the price offered by rich nations to poor nations for the raw goods and agricultural products which they buy from them. The so-called "world market prices," with their wide and sudden fluctuations, force the underdeveloped countries to remain underdeveloped, while the rich nations (by virtue of the materials purchased) transformed by their powerful industries, become richer and richer. This is a dreadful violence in which all of us directly or indirectly participate.

The economy of tomorrow, or rather the day after tomorrow, will be a communitarian economy from which usury will be banished. Haven't exploratory studies already shown that we must one day guarantee a survival income to everyone?

Unfortunately, we are not there yet! This does not, however, justify ignoring these problems and refusing to face up to the economic violence upon which (whether we like it or not) we depend. Accordingly, we must do something.

Members of communities, particularly of Christian communities, should join in all the movements which fight for a new economy; they should support their peaceful protests with all their strength. They should make every possible effort to make people see, to make them understand, and do so by suggesting, persuading and convincing. In those places where the economic battle is being fought, they should use all their strength to influence public opinion so as to bring about the establishment of an economy based principally on need.

Members of communities are ready for such nonviolent action. Indeed in their community life and their sharing of material goods they are concretely achieving, at their level, a prototype of the economic world of tomorrow. They know the transformation of mentality, the constant fraternal dialogue and the nonviolent methods that this demands, but they also know the human balance, justice and security that this brings. It is their duty to begin demonstrating this.

The violence of war is closely linked to economic violence. The first has almost always originated in the second. But members of communities know, like everyone else, that wars solve nothing. The goals of peace, concord and fraternal sharing towards which humanity

131

deeply aspires cannot be attained by such a means. Members of communities, accustomed as they are to overcoming their differences by active nonviolent means, know that this is the only way to reach a general understanding among men and to achieve the common good.

By this very fact communities are the ideal seedbeds for world peace. They should realize this and promote the peaceful resolution of all differences between nations, races and the present classes of society. They should come out of themselves.

They should contact those who determine national and international policy and explain to them the simple things they ignore, show them the faults of their economic and political system and suggest humane solutions to differences. They should participate in all organizations which oppose war and armed conflicts and stir up public opinion which weighs most effectively on the decisions of politicians. Members of communities should press in every possible way for disarmament and the substitution of military service by civil service. And in certain cases they should not be afraid to have recourse, with thought and discipline, to civil disobedience and even to become its promoters and organizers of justifiable dissent.

Every vocation brings its responsibility. Those who have discovered the community cannot understand the world except in this communitarian perspective — otherwise their consciences would be betrayed and others would be deprived of a wealth that members of communities have received in order to give them.

Members of communities are the people who grasp better than others the choice which faces man or which will face him soon: absurdity or utopia. They have chosen utopia. They are right because what is utopia today will be reality tomorrow, while what is today's absurdity will be tomorrow's destruction. If only they could understand all the responsibilities, all the dimensions, and all the implications of their choice!

2. The Church as Community and Evangelization

The Principles

The Christian community should help in the construction of the secular city by all that it is and all that it does. But this isn't enough. It should especially proclaim Jesus Christ and draw as many men as possible into itself. Certainly these two aspects are connected and are found reunited in the ultimate kingdom of the Lord — where there will no longer be a distinction between the natural and the supernatural orders. And even if the one is not found without the other in the Christian community here below, we still must distinguish the two orders in our progress towards the unique goal.

The evangelization of the world is an internal need and pressing duty. In the conciliar decree *The Apostolate and the Laity* we read for example:

The mission of the Church concerns the salvation of men, which is to be achieved by belief in Christ and by his grace. Hence the apostolate of the Church and of all her members is primarily designed to manifest Christ's message by words and deeds and to communicate his grace to the world. . . .

There are innumerable opportunities open to the laity for the exercise of their apostolate of making the gospel known and men holy. The very testimony of the Christian life, and good works done in a super-

133

natural spirit, have the power to draw men to belief and to God; for the Lord says, "Even so let your light shine before men, in order that they may see your good works and give glory to your Father in heaven" (Mt 5:16).

However, an apostolate of this kind does not consist only in the witness of one's way of life; a true apostle looks for opportunities to announce Christ by words addressed either to nonbelievers with a view to leading them to faith, or to believers with a view to instructing and strengthening them, and motivating them towards a more fervent life. "For the love of Christ impels us" (2 Cor 5:14), and the words of the Apostle should echo in every Christian heart: "For woe to me if I do not preach the gospel" (1 Cor 9:16) (no. 6).

. . . True apostles, however, are not content with this activity alone, but look for the opportunity to announce Christ to their neighbors through the spoken word as well. For there are many persons who can hear the gospel and recognize Christ only through the laity who live near them (no. 13).

Everyone has heard the wisecrack of a theologian: "In the vocabulary of the apostolate we've spoken of conquest, then of witness, then of presence, the only thing left is to speak of absence." The Council, for its part, speaks frankly of evangelization. We are surely very far from conquest but neither presence nor witness is enough — we must proclaim Jesus Christ not in order to conquer but to serve. It is a question of love. How can we avoid wanting others to profit by the good news of salvation that has been revealed to us? This isn't a matter of proselytizing but rather the expression of authentic altruism. And if they do not accept our proclamation of

134

the good news we will be quiet, but we will nonetheless continue to love. . . .

The Community's Work of Evangelization

I would like to say a few words on the work of evangelization seen in relation to the Christian community which is its source and soul.

Shouldn't we try to avoid the excessive separation of the lay apostolate and the apostolate of priests? In fact, the apostolate concerns the whole Christian community and each one of its members whether or not they have a hierarchical office. A sort of stratification and the formation of castes and classes (there's that word again!) that we call episcopate, clergy and laity, have been caused by the "decommunitarization" of the Church. . . . Most assuredly it is Christ's will that in each community there be members who have no hierarchical office, others who are deacons, others who are priests and one of them who is the bishop, but a member of the hierarchy remains first of all a brother among his brethren, bound to them, burdened by the same problems, the same difficulties and supported by them just as they are supported by him. And it is the community as such, with the bishops as its head, which has received the mandate to evangelize those who do not belong to it. And the great community of communities, the Church, has received the mandate to evangelize the world. This mission of evangelization rests on the communities and on all the community members from the moment that they are baptized and confirmed.

The bishop who directs the life of the community will also direct the work of the apostolate but he will keep in mind that evangelization is a mission where the charisms of Christians and the freedom of the Spirit are especially operative. Because the bishop and priests are absorbed in serving the community and catechumens, they are sometimes obliged not to participate in other men's employment and therefore they become somewhat isolated and out of contact with the different milieux which make up the world of men. But this isn't necessarily so. Bishops and priests are not monks. It *can* happen that their service of the community allows them to have a working life which keeps them just as much in touch with the world as their brethren who do not have a hierarchical office. Therefore, let's not be too systematic and let's not say these apostolic tasks are for ordinary Christians and these other tasks for priests. No, the work of evangelizing the world is incumbent on communities as such and on the community of communities.

On the subject of the evangelical reality of the Christian community in the world, there exist some ideas which seem to me erroneous. I would like to say a few words about them.

What is said almost amounts to this: The world is involved in a process of "socialization" which cannot be neglected. One of the more important characteristics of this phenomenon is the destruction of deep human relationships between individuals for the sake of a network of "secondary relations" — on the work scene, in restaurants, movie theaters, stores, placement offices, medical services, etc. These settings don't need personal relationships or mutual knowing — it is a matter of "society" pure and simple. There is no community anymore except the family. Therefore, to evangelize the world, the Church should take the world as its model and give up its community character. The parish community especially has no value other than to distribute the word of God and the sacraments. Except for these things the

Church is elsewhere — that is, in some effort of Catholic action whether in a work or recreational setting, in some charitable or relief service or in some health institution, etc.

If the analyses on which these statements are based are to the point and solid, the conclusions deduced from them seem to me false. In fact, the process of "socialization" is not an end but a stage and it doesn't satisfy man. And as long as men stay at the stage of socialization, their families and they themselves will be discontent. It has been written that today the only community man has is his family. This is very often the truth. But we musn't leave it at that and take this as normal and viable. Indeed, the moment we pass from the community to organizational life we endanger the basic community which is the family — the statistics are there to prove it.

Moreover, when we look closely we see men trying to form themselves into communities even, and perhaps especially, in the big cities. In an anonymous and mobile society man seeks roots, he tries to re-create a network of primary relationships where his real life will be situated and where he will be entirely himself. Why? Because he wants to save himself.

Therefore, to evangelize a changing world the Church ought primarily to respect deeply her own sociological reality (which is all the more human because it is divine) and remain a community as her founder willed. And if she has lost much of her communitarian character, it is urgent that she recover it in its fullness. I certainly do not want to say that the geographical parish, even if renewed, can always and everywhere play the role of the base community but only that Christians need a base community (geographical or otherwise) where they can all join in hearing the word of God, where they can celebrate the Eucharist together, eat together sometimes, share spiritually and materially and be happy together. Only in this way will they be able to offer themselves to the world not only as Christians (which isn't of much importance) but as Christians who are such inasmuch as they are members of a community.

Catholic Action

As members of authentic communities Christians should be present everywhere there are men not only to work with them in the construction of the secular city but to witness to Christ by their lives. And this witness and this proclamation of the gospel is not only an individual effort but also a collective, concerted and organized activity — it is, in particular, Catholic action.

Consequently, Christians who belong to different base communities but who work in the same factory, the same area or form part of some particular milieu meet together, organize and prepare for apostolic action in this factory, this area or this milieu. They don't do this by cutting themselves off from their base communities but on the contrary they are sent by these and report their activities to them.

In itself the base community is socially heterogeneous. Its members belong to all sorts of categories or classes. And the fact that, different as they are one from the other, they share spiritually and materially is perhaps the most extraordinary sign that they can give the world.

We must then see in principle that a specialized Catholic action group does not become a base community for its members — unless in certain cases it is only a step towards the reconstruction of real communities. For I confess that in speaking of base communities, I have presented an idea which is not yet sufficiently
138

actualized. In many cases base communities, parishes which are geographic or otherwise, still need to be established. And Catholic action should labor at this work of the first order. On the one hand, we can say that if Catholic action hasn't been fruitful this is precisely because it has lacked roots. Because it hasn't come out of real communities, it hasn't had a concrete point of departure or support, and hasn't known where to lead the men who have received its message. But, on the other hand, it has induced many Christians to encounter one another and by meeting together, reading scripture, praying and meditating on their apostolic action, to know one another and to share with one another. If they want to give full value to these relationships and this sharing, they will move toward the community and if, going beyond the limits of their specialization, they start to share with others, they will lay down the foundations of a community of the Church. The new Catholic action which we need will come from authentic communities of the Church.

The Missions

In speaking of evangelization I have emphasized the role of Catholic action. We must say a special word about the missions. While in principle Catholic action and the ordinary apostolate proceed from existing communities in order to make these grow, missionary work consists in the foundation of new communities by old communities.

Therefore, let missionaries as God's co-workers, raise up congregations of the faithful who will walk in a manner worthy of the vocation to which they have been called, and will exercise the priestly, prophetic,

139

and royal office which God has entrusted to them. In this way, the Christian community becomes a sign of God's presence in the world. For by reason of the Eucharistic Sacrifice, this community is ceaselessly on the way with Christ to the Father. Carefully nourished on the word of God, it bears witness to Christ. And, finally, it walks in love and glows with an apostolic spirit.

From the very start, the Christian community should be so formed that it can provide for its own necessities in so far as this is possible (Council decree on *The Missionary Activity of the Church,* no. 15).

A mission is, strictly speaking, the sending of one or more members outside the community to found a new community elsewhere with the people to whom they are sent. The missionaries, who may be laymen or priests, are then clearly separated from their base community so that they may become Jews with the Jews and Greeks with the Greeks in order to bring about the creation of new Christian communities. Within these communities, they will be members in exactly the same way as the people to whom they are sent. It may happen that they will be sent by this new community to found still another community, etc., but the mission of itinerant founders of communities is exceptional in the Church, even though it is necessary and important.

In any case, the work of evangelization, as we can see, presupposes communities and leads back to these communities or causes the creation of communities. The apostolate is the means; the community is the end — the community of the kingdom of heaven — but also the community of the pilgrim Church which is the beginning of the heavenly kingdom.

CONCLUSION

Today any human group that doesn't look ahead condemns itself to wither or even disappear. It is the same with the Church. The future assuredly is God's, but God speaks to the Church today for the construction of the Church of tomorrow. We must pay attention to these calls from the Lord and sense the direction in which the breath of the Spirit blows. We must detect this thrust of life to draw a likeness of the Church of the year 2000 and the year 2051. We must. How can we move towards a goal if we don't have at least an idea of the goal to be reached? How can the infant Church grow if it doesn't have in itself a picture of the adult Church?

I wanted to sketch a likeness. It is, I grant, imperfect and still blurred, but perhaps it will allow the reader to make a few steps in the right direction. I wish him with all my heart the courage he needs to move decisively towards the goal, the realism he needs to size up the present situation and the prudence he needs to completely preserve truth and love.

It is well understood that the construction of a Church as community poses many problems. The *Centre Communautaire International* 135, rue Bemel, Bruxelles 15, Belgique, founded in February, 1965, is an organization whose purpose is the study and fostering of community life. It can doubtlessly help you because it seeks out and gathers all the information on community experiments, studies them, brings different communities together and from this offers doctrinal and practical advice on community life. Out of our efforts and our achievements, our groping, our difficulties and our errors, the new Church of tomorrow will be able to rise.

NOTES

1 M. H. Vicaire, O.P. *L'imitation des apotres,* Paris, ed. du Cerf, 1963.

2 See H. Dussourd, *Au meme pot, au meme feu,* Moulins, obtainable from the author; *La communaute des Boisseau, Courrier Communautaire International,* 2e annee, no. 3, pp. 30-34.

3 C. Lugon, *La Republique communiste chretienne des Guaranis,* Paris, ed. Ouvrieres, 1949.

4 Many descriptions of modern Christian communities can be found in the periodical *Courrier Communautaire International.*

5 D. Bonhoeffer, *De la vie communautaire,* ed. Delachaux et Niestle, 1955, p. 11f.

6 "Jamaa," loosely speaking, means family. This term designates the small communities of the Church which have arisen outside the tribal milieu in the Congo. The Africans who belong to them have discovered the truth about their fraternity in Christ. They have understood that Jesus gives the same life to each of them and that they communicate it to one another. Many bishops see in the Jamaa the greatest hope for the Christianization of Black Africa.

7 In many groups and especially in some communities, a revision of life is practiced which has the appearance of a "confession" (in the original sense of the word), of a sharing in common before the Lord. I have participated in such confessions many times. After they are finished, all say the Confiteor ("I confess to God") and the priest pronounces the two absolutions which follow it. In the opinion of those taking part, it is not so much a question of the sacrament of penance as a sort of presacramental celebration. Couldn't theologians study the exact essence of this sharing together? Might this not be a way to restore the sacrament of penance? Can we hope that someday such confessions made in small communities will be ratified by sacramental absolution, while

142

private confession remains available to everyone? This is simply a request to the theologians to respectfully observe a spiritual phenomenon being lived right now in many communities and to present their conclusions eventually to the bishops.

8 These texts are quoted from R. Carpentier, etc., *L'Eveque et la vie religieuse consacree,* in *L'Episcopat et l'Eglise universelle,* coll. Unam Sanctam, Paris, ed. du Cerf, 1962.

9 See J. N. Gatheron, *L'usure devorante,* Paris, ed. Ouvrieres, 1963.

10 R. Carpentier, *La communaute chretienne dans l'histoire,* review *Courrier Communautaire International,* December 15, 1966, pp. 48-50.

11 D. Chenu, *L'economie du 20e siecle et la vertu de la Promesse,* Encyclopedie Francaise, t. IX, ch. III.

12 This is taken from the first draft of *Schema 13,* art. 23, no. 4, p. 27. The amendment which the bishops signed concerned this text.

13 F. Petit, La vie commune des clercs, review *Courrier Communautaire International,* Vol. 1, no. 13, pp. 20-32.

14 Among the most remarkable examples of the integration of the religious life into the ordinary community we must mention "la Poudriere." Right in the center of Bruxelles, this community groups together five Oblates of Mary Immaculate, some families with children, some unmarried persons, in all almost 50 people.

15 G. Minette de Tillesse, *L'Eglise et le monde,* in *Irenikon,* T. XXXVIII, no. 2, Chevetogne, 1965, p. 172.

16 Cf. *La charte federaliste;* M. ORBAN, *Structures economiques en democratie federale,* in the review *Courrier Communautaire International,* Vol. 1, no. 5.